MW01105437

Write down one thing you want to do before you die:

PRAISE FOR

live
• YOUR
list

"I'm sorry James Ryan Eller wrote a book??? As in, my mean older cousin who liked to make me cry as a pre teen. That guy???? Nope, sorry. I don't think I want to read that book. Nah, you are right. He isn't that guy anymore. The guy who wrote this book is now an encourager and a person who positively molds me daily. Yeah, ok. That guy could write a good book."

| *Cousin Amy*

"In this book, there are pages. On these pages are words. Some of those words will probably resonate with you. I don't really know your personality. I guess if you are boring, you will probably dislike this book. If you don't want to do anything with your life, just don't buy the book, you loser. Go play video games and let someone more important read this."

| *Kyle the Intern*

"I'm not sure what you're talking about. A book review? No thank you. Ask someone else."

| *Random dude in Walmart*

"The author of this book does an incredible job at captivating audiences and leading people into growth and insight. He has dedicated his life to helping others reach their full potential. He extends his influence in providing this resource. Ryan lives his life in a thoughtful, intentional, and generous way. In the spirit of authenticity and to further provide an example of how to live life generously and intentionally he has selflessly devoted half of all proceeds from this book to his loving twin sister. Do not hesitate to buy this book or to hold him accountable to this generous act."

| *Melissa Hall, PhD, LPC, NCC, CFLE*

live
. YOUR
list

"I've watched as my son walked with lions, ran a Marathon around the Great Wall of China, learned to juggle, stepped into a -300 degree tube, and helped bring solar power to an African school. Living Your List isn't just knocking down a to-do list for Ryan Eller, it's a passion that has caused this mother to cheer him on while holding her breath that his next list item won't kill him. If you want to read a book that will launch you into a *Live Your List* life (and scare your mom to death), this book is exactly what you need."

Suzanne (Suzie) Eller, international speaker,
bestselling author, Living Free Together Ministries,
and mother of Ryan Eller

"This book is engaging, inspiring, and will absolutely change your life. I adore everything about it and can't wait to see the wonderful things people will go and do after reading it. I look forward to the significant pay raise I will receive after the time and effort I put into helping create the most amazing piece of literature you've ever read."

Rachel Mayo, Ryan's Assistant

"I have traveled to over 50 countries, to almost every US state, and live internationally for many years. I have jumped out of planes, hung out with celebrities, and been (wrongly) accused of being a terrorist. I have done some amazing things in my life, but in all things Ryan Eller is my superior. He even asked me to write this testimonial over five times and I never did, so he is better at this than me too."

Zach the Chemical Engineer

"Hey! This looks like a book."

Philip, the New Intern

"This is the greatest book in the history of books. The author is tall, dark, and handsome with an incredible wit. The lessons you learn in this book will be the greatest lessons you will ever learn in your entire life. I am thankful for his life."

Ryan Eller, Author of Live Your List

live
.YOUR
list

HOW TO ACHIEVE YOUR DREAMS, MAKE A DIFFERENCE,

PURSUE YOUR PURPOSE, AND RIDE AN ELEPHANT AT THE SAME TIME

RYAN ELLER

live
.YOUR
list

First edition published
December 2017

Book Design by Amanda Mazzo, Mazzo Media

Printed in China
Edited by Rachel Mayo

Archival and family photographs
courtesy of Ryan Eller

If you read this, email Ryan and he will send you a gift.

ISBN # 978-0-9997111-0-1

When I was a senior in college I was named "Outstanding Male Senior" - which meant I was the most outstanding male student on campus (I am sure you picked up on that). When I gave my award speech to the thousands tens of people in the crowd, I mentioned that one of the reasons I have had any amount of success in my life is because I have been fortunate to be surrounded by successful people.

People that have encouraged me, challenged me, and shown me the path to success.

Here is a short list of the people who have helped me live my list:

Kristin
Jane Bane
Bubs Mcgee
GaGa
Big Dad
Leslo
Dr. Hall
Josh
Stevo-Dacorino
Ma
Pa
Murr
Morrison Crew
Cousin Amy
The Mayos
Neha
Kyle the Intern
Philip the New Intern
Lucy Pup
Miss Congeniality
Zachy
Roy Boy
The White House
Shelby the Girl Intern
Stephinfection
Dana E
NSU
LXA
Dr. Aldridge
Bre Bre
Nodnarb & DDot
Walker
Adneys
Fenskas

Acuff Nation
Tulsa 5 Club
Loyd & Jake
Garbo & Letta
The Welch Crew
SWASAP
Obi Wan
Cupcake
The Ghelanis
My Littles
Obama
Chopstick
DBallard
Clay Bennett
Cousin Austin
The Neighbors
Bevo & Shade
#TRIOWorks
Flatt
The Blakemore
My Second College Roommate
Toosh
Bandit
The Northeastern Crew
The Waterslide
Nick Collison
Firepower Youth
Pastor Rose
Ralphie & Paige
Mubita C Nawa the Magnificent
Uncle Weeze
Benji & Alex
Mark & Nate
Frittsee

Thomas
Squarehead
Double J and Kyle Shepard
The Kings
Paco
Peakers
Randy Reibenstein
The Train Station
Britches
Pledge Class of 2005
WMCIII
The '01 Initiates
The OKC Thunder
Okies from Muskogee
Sam Bracken
Power Deb
Red Rattlers
Fleet Feet Tulsa
Elm Grove Fire Department
Oskar Schindler
Sheila
Gray Sheila
Hot Shots Part Deux
Momma Murr
Kent and Viv
M1A
Merle Haggard
Creek Nation
PLC
Grandmother Franklin
Motivational Posters
The Nickells
Megmonds
Live Your List Nation

live
YOUR
list

FORWARD BY JERROD MURR

A long, long, time ago I can still remember that magical movie.

It was *Miss Congeniality* (thank you, Sandra Bullock), and it was the start of one of the greatest friendships of my life.

It is funny how strongly events happening right now shape the rest of our lives. How a terrible double date (the *Miss Congeniality* one) can eventually lead to a lifelong brag buddy, business partner, and world traveling companion. You see, the decisions we make today drastically dictate what our life will be tomorrow.

That is what *Live Your List* is all about.

We must be intentional about our decisions or life just happens, we miss it.

I have had the rare privilege of seeing Ryan's entire journey. I knew him in high school and college. I knew single Ryan and married Ryan. I knew Ryan before he had children and now I know Ryan the father. Most importantly, I knew Ryan before he adopted the *Live Your List* mindset, and I have seen his life in action ever since. The difference is undeniable.

Ryan Eller is one of the most impressive people I know. His ability to connect with others is unparalleled. The life he lives is extraordinary. I watch it on social media and in person and I am challenged. Ryan challenges me to live a better life. It is not in a "my-life-is-better-than-yours" type of challenge that creates competition. It is more of an invitation. Ryan challenges me to live a better life by inviting me to join him.

Ryan is an outstanding human being. This inspires me. When we think of remarkable people, we tend to assume they are born this way. The great leaders of the past, the great influencers of history, seem to have an other-worldly characteristic about them that normal people like you and me just do not possess. In watching Ryan, this is not true. Ryan is one of those great leaders, one of those amazing influencers, but he is normal, approachable, like you and me. This is what inspires me. He has never let his failures trap him or his flaws define him. He continues to grow, and get better. He continues to live his list. Every day I see him travel the world, meet the people of this world, and change this world. He gives me hope that I can do the same thing.

Ryan celebrates others. This may be his secret weapon. Ryan has this incredible ability to connect with others and make them feel important and valued. I think it is because he honestly feels that way. Ryan values people. He listens. He cheers people on. He likes your posts, and shares your stories. I am truly humbled to be his friend. He makes me want to be a better friend.

The stories you are about to hear are true. I hope you learn from them. Some of them are strong warnings of what can happen when you don't try your best. Others are inspirational nuggets of the possibilities that exist in this wonderful world of ours. As you hear the true tales from the life of Ryan (and his friends), I hope that you heed the warnings, and adopt the hope. You truly can do great things in this world, if you work hard, and give it your best effort.

Dream big.
Dare greatly.
Live Your List.

TABLE OF CONTENTS

live
.your
list

HOW TO ACHIEVE YOUR DREAMS, MAKE A DIFFERENCE,

PURSUE YOUR PURPOSE, AND RIDE AN ELEPHANT AT THE SAME TIME

RYAN ELLER

I first knew my life was starting to change while lying on my stomach in China. A five-foot tall woman was lighting fishbowls on fire before she placed them on my back. I wasn't sure if I was being tortured, but I knew I had officially been following my dream to *Live My List*.

I spoke zero Mandarin, and this lady spoke very little English. We had wandered our way into the massage parlor without knowing that you had to be extremely careful when choosing a parlor. Apparently massage parlor means something completely different in China than it does in the United States.*

However, we chose wisely and ended up in a salon that offered two-hour long massages, and each person had two massage therapists. We were asked to dress up in thick velvet robes and plush slippers before we hopped into a co-ed sauna.

* Unless that is how you think of massage parlors. Then it means exactly the same thing.

It was strange to be in a steamy room with ten older Chinese people, but not nearly as strange for us as it was for them.

You would have thought we were aliens. I had to stoop down to enter the door, and my 6-foot-2, 200-pound frame took almost an entire bench. The Chinese sat three people on a bench. The large American sat one. They had stripped their robes and were wearing the see-through underwear that the salon provided. We were still modestly in our robes.

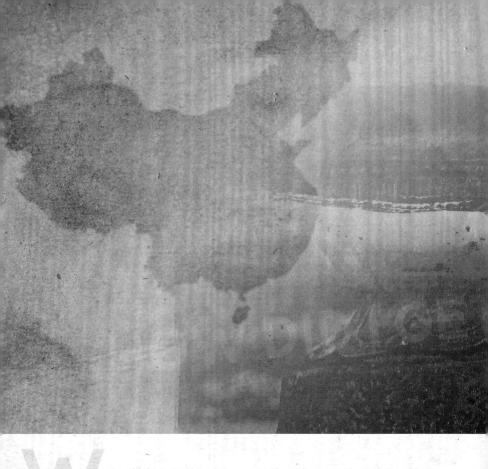

We saw many odd things in China. We were in Zhengzhou, an industrial city with very little tourism. We said that there were two parts of China – tourist China and real China. Real China had small animals hanging in the side street markets. The toddlers didn't wear diapers, instead they wore pants that had slits in the crotch so they could go to the bathroom wherever they wanted. There were random chickens that would walk around in the middle of a city of ten million.

Of all of the odd things we saw in China, the see-through underwear was the oddest. It was unusually small and completely see-through. They served no purpose other than to make the American visitors feel completely uncomfortable.

After a few minutes of awkwardness, the sauna steam enveloped us and provided a screen of relaxation amongst the group. When our sauna time was finished, the massage therapists led us into a candlelit room playing relaxing music that sounded like there was a bubbling stream running through the middle of the massage tables.

The next two hours were amazing. One masseuse focused on massaging my feet while the other massaged my upper body. I had no idea how these little women could apply so much force into my back. It felt like a jackhammer knocking away at my sore spots. I'm pretty sure they could have helped fix roads with those hands. I was beat up, but completely relaxed at the same time.

After the massage, my masseuse asked me something in very broken English. I was almost asleep at this point, so I had to focus to understand what she was saying.

"You want Chinese cupping?"

"What"

"Chinese cupping."

"Um, cupping?"

"Remove negative Chi. Very good for you."

I didn't know what she was talking about, but if she said it was good for me, I was going to do it. I think this lady could have punched me in the face and taken all of my money and I would have been thankful. She could have even convinced me to buy some see-through underwear.

I agreed to let her try the Chinese cupping on me without even knowing what she was going to do. We might have accidentally stumbled into one of the sketchy Chinese massage parlors we had been warned about, but it was too late to back out now. If I could have been in a state of mind to be worried, I would have been sweating bullets.

I was still dazed as she rolled out a cart that held about 30 fishbowls and strangely, a torch! A torch? What was that for? Did she need more light? Was there a journey involved during this massage? Did she plan on entering a tunnel to drink water out of the Holy Grail?

Either way I was **NERVOUS.**

She took a smelly oil and rubbed it all over my back. Alright, now I get it. She is going to light my back on fire. This is the end for me. This was a trap for tourists. The Chinese were smart, they wanted to lure you into ultimate relaxation before they burned you to a crisp. They made you so relaxed that you couldn't even fight back when they started to baste you like a turkey.

As I was crying for help, she took the torch and stuck it on the inside of one of the fishbowls on the cart. She lowered the torch and fishbowl near my back, removed the torch, and then stuck the bowl right on my shoulder. The fire had sucked all of the oxygen out of the bowl making it a strong suction cup.

The fishbowl that sat on my shoulder started to suck my flesh further and further inside of the glass. It hurt. Not a small amount of hurt, but a large amount of hurt. Imagine someone pulling the skin on your shoulder into a ring and then pulling it constantly through the ring. That's what I felt like. I am not going to lie to you fine folks, I cried.

It wasn't sobbing crying, but tough man crying. You know, when a guy bites their lower lip as a single tear rolls down their cheek, dropping onto the floor like a dramatic drop of rain. Before the tear could even hit the ground, the masseuse set another fishbowl on my back. This time on my lower back.

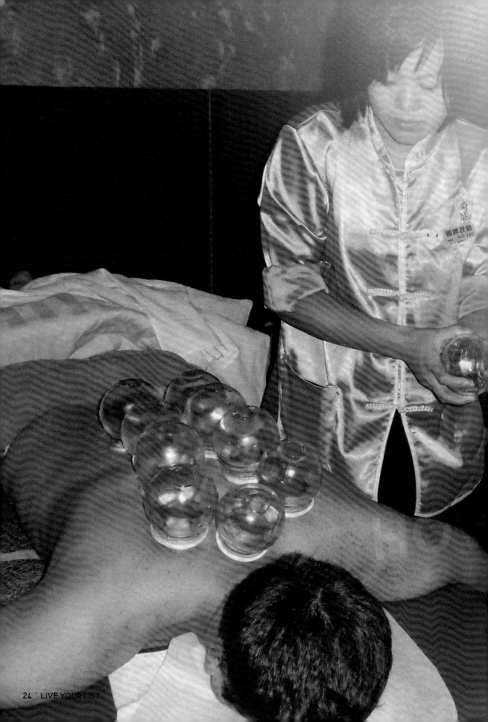

If you thought shoulder skin seeping into a hot fishbowl was painful, you clearly haven't had one placed on your lower back. This Chinese torturer was just getting started. Within five minutes, she had placed 30 fishbowls of pain all over my back.

I mean, who else had ever experienced this form of slow torture? I was out of my comfort zone to say the least, but I felt alive. **I felt strong. I felt like I was living life to the fullest.**

I HAD STARTED TO LIVE MY LIST.

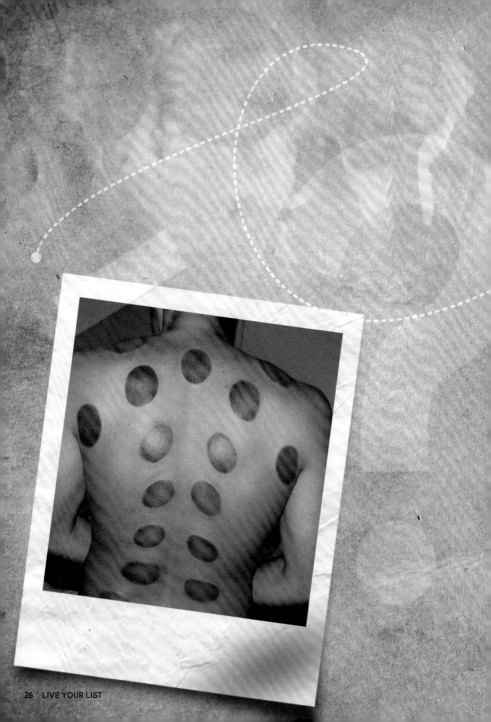

HOW DID I GET HERE?

If you *Live Your List*, you are taking control of your destiny. You are living an inspired life full of adventure and intrigue as a life-long learner. The *Live Your List* philosophy includes Bucket Lists, IDs and ACT Goals, and defining your purpose. It's about dreams, both great and small. It is a mindset. It is a way of life.

It is more than getting set on fire in China, and it was as if the heat searing into my back had lit a fire of understanding about my life. I had been on a journey of self-discovery for many years.

It was then, however, that I started to wonder how I had gotten myself into this position. What decision had I made that led me to being lit on fire in China? I have heard that people's lives flash before their eyes right before they die. I wasn't sure if this was one of those moments, but I started to review my life nonetheless.

JULY 9, 1983
Born in
Muskogee, OK

JUNE 1986
Started working on the
family dairy farm

1983

DECEMBER 23, 1983
First taste of cookies;
forever hooked

1985

MAY 14, 1985
Filled up a bucket
with a hose

1986

AUGUST 23, 1988
Started school

19

AUGUST 1998
Hit by drunk driver; had to
relearn how to walk

AUGUST 1999
Took the next
Eller Ear Pic

1996

1998

1999

2

MAY 1998
Went to the state track
meet in the 800m dash

MAY 1999
Ran first track meet
after wreck; came in last

FEBRUARY 1996
Middle School girlfriend
broke up with me at
Valentine's Dance

IN REVIEW

1990

1993

1995

AUGUST 24, 1988
Got in trouble for
talking to friends

JUNE 1993
Took the famed
"Ear Picture"

MARCH 1990
Traveled to Jamaica
on a missions trip

APRIL 16, 1995
Won first place in the
Hilldale Middle School
Science Fair

JULY 2002
Ate an entire
birthday cake

MAY 2003
Removed from
PLC Scholarship

MAY 2001
Graduated from
Hilldale High School

2001

2002

2003

FEBRUARY 2000
Milk-A-Thon;
Did not go well

AUGUST 2001
Started at
Northeastern
State University
as a President's
Leadership
Class Scholar

29

MAY 2006
Graduated College &
Went on First Date
with Kristin

APRIL 2004
Wrote Bucket List in NYC

2004

2005

2006

20

FEBRUARY 2005
Danced with
Miss America

JANUARY 2013
Kissed Kristin on
top of the Eiffel Tower

NOVEMBER 2011
Jane was Born

2011

2012

2013

2

SEPTEMBER 2012
Won a game show

IN REVIEW

MARCH 2008
Married the hottest
woman on the planet

OCTOBER 2010
Visited the Great Wall
of China

7 **2008** **2009** **2010**

JUNE 2007
Proposed on Hot
Air Balloon

APRIL 2009
Completed OKC
Marathon

OCTOBER 2017
Almost got eaten
by a lion in Africa

NOVEMBER 2015
Caleb was Born

4 **2015** **2016** **2017**

OCTOBER 2014
Stood upon
a glacier

OCTOBER 2016
Visited all 50
US States

DECEMBER 2017
Published the
Live Your List Book

After reading through those last few pages, you might be asking yourself a few questions:

> **How has Ryan always been so handsome?***
> **Why does this guy think he is so handsome?**
> **How does he know what I am thinking?**
> **Why is the calf on page 24 bucktoothed?**
> **Why did I just read these last few pages?**

I shared my life in review with you for a few reasons, but primarily to show you that an average kid born into an average family with average ability has been able to do some amazing things in his life.

I was not born into money, I wasn't the best student in class, and life has not always been easy - but I am not deterred. I have learned that if I set goals for my life, manage my time, and pursue my purpose I will be able to accomplish amazing things...and most importantly, I will be able to help others do the same.

So that is what *Live Your List* is about. Taking advantage of the opportunities you've been given to make a difference in the world. In the following pages I will walk you through the Seven Levels to *Live Your List*. It is a system that has helped me find my purpose, travel the world, and multiply my gifts.

My hope is that you will find value in my words.** Take the time to fill out the worksheets in this book and share your ideas with others. If you are enjoying this book feel free to tweet us *@Live_Your_List* or *@ryan_eller*. I promise I will tweet you back.

So... without further ado, here is the story of a young kid from rural Oklahoma that ended up winning a game show, dancing with Miss America, walking a length of the Great Wall of China, and marrying the hottest person he had ever met...

---

* I didn't ask that last question!
** And not be bored.

live YOUR list

TAKE PERSONAL RESPONSIBILITY

CREATE LISTS

WHAT IS YOUR ID

CHART YOUR TIME

FIND YOUR VERB

PARLAY

MULTIPLY

GROWING UP ON A
DAIRY FARM

How did a kid who grew up on a dairy farm on the plains of Oklahoma end up on fire in China? When we were little kids, we didn't travel much further than end of our farm. As "Professional Utter Handlers," that's what you call dairy farmers, my mom and dad milked cows twice a day, every day, regardless of weather, holiday, or occasion.

I can remember my parents going to dairy conventions from time-to-time to amazing vacation destinations like Idaho Falls, Idaho and Oshkosh, Wisconsin, but there was little opportunity to travel to exotic destinations like China. Exploration, however, was always important to our little family, even when we were young.

Often while dad was busy bailing hay, mom would take my two sisters and me on journeys through the pastures. We had all of the things a kid would need to explore: thick woods with tall trees, bail yards with hidden tunnels through the hay, and even a junk pit full of trash and old cars.

Mom would help us create stories about our journeys to the junk pit. We would even get to take a piece of junk home as our prize.* We thought junk was the greatest thing ever. I once took a cow leg bone I found in the dump to kindergarten Show and Tell as one of my prized possessions. Even though we weren't swimming in gold coins like Scrooge McDuck, my parents worked very hard to nurture our sense of adventure.

I can remember my mom saying,

> **"We are all the same, except for the things we read, the places we go, and the people we know. One day you will have the chance to travel the world and meet amazing people. When that time comes take advantage of the opportunity."**

* Looking back. we might have been poor.

I didn't quite understand it at the time, but I am pretty sure my sisters picked up on it right away. My older sister, Leslie, was only 19 months older than me, but she was extremely intelligent. Both mom and dad would talk to Leslie like an adult because she could hold an adult conversation.

I can remember Leslie reciting all of the lines of the *Wizard of Oz* with her baby dolls playing the different roles. She was barely four years old and had memorized an entire movie. She often took adults by surprise when they would ask her a childish question and they would get an adult response.

Leslie would carefully explain things to my sister Melissa and me. Melissa and I were twins, and teammates from the beginning. There were things I could do better than her, and things she could do better than me, but together we were unstoppable.

Once, when we were still in diapers, Melissa and I somehow climbed a tree and ended up on top of the barn. My dad and grandpa were supposed to be watching us, but didn't notice us until they heard little footsteps on top of the barn. They ran to look on top and we were sitting on the edge of the barn kicking our feet.

We were adventurous in every manner. As kindergarteners, the bus driver dropped us off at the farm instead of the babysitter's house. Instead of being scared, we broke into our house. It is one of my earliest memories, but I distinctly remember helping Melissa climb through a very small window that was above the washer and dryer in our little farmhouse. She hopped on the dryer, unlocked the door, and let me inside.

When mom and Leslie finally found us, we were sitting on the floor watching cartoons while eating peanut butter and jelly sandwiches. Mom was scared and I just didn't understand. I said,

"BUT MOM, IT IS 2:30. WHY WOULDN'T WE BE WATCHING CARTOONS RIGHT NOW?"

Leslie helped us understand that we were supposed to be frightened after being alone. That's what made the three of us such a good team. Melissa and I were fearless adventurers, and Leslie was a source of wisdom and understanding as our translator.

As much as my parents nurtured our sense of adventure, they also encouraged us to take responsibility for our lives. This was particularly hard for me because at some point in our lives our little team of three turned into a team of two against one.

I love my sisters, and it is probably unfair for me to describe their treatment towards me as two against one, but I am writing this story. Check out their autobiographies some day to see if I am telling the truth.

The problem with the two against one system was that it was unfair one against one. Both of my sisters were smarter than me. I am not throwing myself under the bus, I am smarter than most. I have a couple college degrees, run my own business, and was smart enough to marry my wife. However, Leslie is now an attorney and Melissa has her PhD. They both have doctorates. Melissa somehow even convinced me to call her Dr. Melissa.

Melissa was the master influencer. She was the queen of getting you to do things she wanted you to do while making you think you were the one who was making the decision. Leslie has the quickest brain of anyone I have ever met. She has a unique ability to process information and come to a sensible conclusion faster than a computer. It is almost a superpower.

Melissa and Leslie would consistently get me to do things I didn't want to do and make me think I actually wanted to do it. It always started the same way, with a challenge.

There were several times where I found myself confidently strutting around the house wearing makeup and dressed like a cow. Melissa and Leslie would be taking pictures of me laughing the whole time. I remember thinking that they were the ridiculous ones, but somehow they had tricked me into this situation.

Can I take a moment and just be thankful that social media wasn't around during my childhood? I'm pretty sure Leslie and Melissa would have somehow convinced me to put the pictures online. Someday I would want to have done something important and the interviewers would look through my Facebook and see me dressed up like a cow.

At some point while I was dressed up I would stop and wonder how I got myself into this situation. Wait, this started with my sister telling me I couldn't fit into my childhood cow costume. It ended up with me wearing makeup and posing for pictures.

This is the power my sisters had over my inferior intellect. Over the years I cleaned their room, washed their cars, ran their errands, and even bought their gas. They were the masters of ~~manipulation~~ influence.

DID I GET MYSELF
THIS SITUATION?

As I got older I started to pick up on their tricks. When I was a teenager I would get angry with them when I felt like they were teaming up on me. I became known for my temper.

Melissa and I once got into a fight in the hallway outside of our Trigonometry class, and it carried over into the classroom. Melissa would shoot little jabs of insults to me under her breath, and I would yell back at her. The teacher ended up sending me to the principal's office and Melissa didn't get into a lick of trouble.

I just couldn't understand. She was as equally guilty as I was, but because I reacted in such a loud way, I was the one who got in trouble. She even instigated the fight by kicking me into the shin. This wasn't a light love tap kick into my shin. This was the late 90s and Melissa wore Doc Marten's. Doc Marten's were solid as concrete. When she kicked me in the shin my bone bent backwards. It didn't matter though, because no one saw her kick me, they just heard me push her into the locker.

I even got into trouble when I got home. My parents had a policy of punishing us separately. They learned that when the three of us got punished together it always ended up with more fighting afterwards. I don't know what kind of trouble Melissa got into, but I know that I got punished.

I kept telling my parents how unfair it all was. Melissa started this whole fight with the kick heard round the world. My parents kept saying it didn't matter what Melissa did or did not do, it only mattered what I did.

My dad looked me right in the eye and said,

"YOU HAVE TO TAKE 100% RESPONSIBILITY FOR YOUR LIFE.

There are always going to be things you have no control over. It is your reaction that you have control over."

Of course, my reaction to that was even more anger. More anger led to more frustration, which led to more anger. It was a never-ending cycle in which everyone could handle their actions except for me. It wasn't until many years later that my dad's words truly started to impact the way I handled my actions.

It took years of frustration and blaming others to understand what he meant about being 100% responsible for my actions. You would think that my sisters would have given me enough opportunities to take responsibility, but I was hardheaded and didn't learn from them, and it cost me in the long run.

MY [TYPICAL] REACTIONS

Melissa ended up getting her PhD in counseling and psychology and is literally an expert in her field. She once told me that it is OK for me to get upset. For the most part, we can not control how we feel. If something makes us feel sad, we will be sad. If something makes us feel angry, we will be angry. Same can be said for times that we feel annoyed, frustrated, happy, afraid, shy, or hurt.

In all honesty, we have very little control of our emotions. We also have little control on how others treat us, how people make us feel, and how we feel about other people.*

We do have 100% control over one thing, however - our response to our emotions. I can't always control the outside influences that can make me feel angry, but I can control my response to my anger. Let me give you an example:

SCENARIO I:

I am stuck in traffic at the end of a long day and I am already tired. A large truck cuts me off and runs me into the ditch. Other than the harm of the little bit of screeching that I did, both the truck and I are relatively unscathed.

I can have the following reactions:
1. I can yell and curse and scream and throw a fit inside of my car.**
2. I can get out of my car and challenge the driver of the large truck to fisticuffs.
3. I can be thankful I wasn't hurt and show forgiveness to the driver because he is likely to feel as irritated and tired as I feel.

---

* Especially people we find attractive - but that is a different story for an entirely different book.

** Always found this to be an interesting tactic since no one can actually hear me screaming at them!

Which of these options do you think will make me feel best? Well in the short-term, I think I would feel best if I yelled and screamed. I am not sure if I would feel good after I challenged the driver of a large truck to a fist fight!

Option #3 would be the least stressful, most calm, and most productive response. It would also be the most challenging way to respond to that scenario. Let's be honest, when I am in that exact scenario I am an absolute butt. I am mean, angry, and vindictive. That is my reaction when I'm stuck in traffic.

The good news is that we can train ourselves to be aware of our typical reactions and start to exhibit the type of reactions we desire. This is really good if you are stuck in traffic with me in the car.

It is our own response to our emotions that determines how we will eventually be known. Do you want to be known as someone who is quick to anger or easy to forgive? Do you want to be known as someone who is fun and encouraging or someone who is pessimistic and a Debbie Downer?

Step one in this process is to take personal responsibility to the types of reactions you currently display when experiencing different situations.

Fill out the chart below and be 100% honest about how you respond in these different scenarios.

ACTION ➡ REACTION

1 A friend or family member lies to me.   **1** _____

2 My phone cuts out.   **2** _____

3 I am stuck in traffic.   **3** _____

4 I get scared.   **4** _____

5 I am asked to give a speech.   **5** _____

6 I don't like what I see in the mirror.   **6** _____

7 Someone insults me.   **7** _____

8 I am running late.   **8** _____

9 My friend lets me down.   **9** _____

10 I am at a buffet line.   **10** _____

Now that you have taken 100% responsibility for your actions, let's try to choose the desired reactions we would like to have in the same exact situations.

How do you want to react?

ACTION → [DESIRED] REACTION

1 A friend or family member lies to me.

2 My phone cuts out.

3 I am stuck in traffic.

4 I get scared.

5 I am asked to give a speech.

6 I don't like what I see in the mirror.

7 Someone insults me.

8 I am running late.

9 My friend lets me down.

10 I am at a buffet line.

1 _____

2 _____

3 _____

4 _____

5 _____

6 _____

7 _____

8 _____

9 _____

10 _____

Taking personal responsibility for our reactions is just the first step of the *Live Your List* process. We have to take ownership for our entire life. There is a great quote from Louis L'Amour that does a much better job of describing personal responsibility than I ever could.*

> Up to a point a man's life is shaped by environment, heredity, and the movements and changes in the world around him. Then there comes a time when it lies within his grasp to shape the clay of his life into the sort of thing he wishes to be. Only the weak blame parents, their race, their times, lack of good fortune, or the quirks of fate. Everyone has it within his power to say, 'This I am today; that I will be tomorrow.' The wish, however, must be implemented by deeds. —Louis L'Amour

* Which is why he wrote 700 gazillion books and I have only written one

Let's break this quote down line by line —

> **Up to a point a man's life is shaped by environment, heredity, and the movements and changes in the world around him.** *

In the beginning part of our life we are mostly affected by things outside of our control. We may be born to jerks for parents, grow up poor, weak, or slow. We may also be born tall, dark, handsome, and smart to rich parents. The world will change around us and affect who we are as people.

> **Then there comes a time when it lies within his grasp to shape the clay of his life into the sort of thing he wishes to be.**

Regardless of the situations we were born into, there becomes a point in which we must take control of our destiny. We are like an unfinished mound of clay. Of course we have been shaped up to a point, but we are a big fat mound of clay that needs to be shaped.**

* I would argue that this is not just a quote for men, but for women too. Come on Louis, be progressive.

**By no means am I calling any of you a big fat mound of clay - it's metaphorical - unless you are a big mound of clay, then I am sorry

> **Only the weak blame parents, their race, their times, lack of good fortune, or the quirks of fate.**

As mentioned earlier, we are initially shaped by things out of our control. And then there becomes a point when we take personal responsibility for our life.* Once we take control of our life we can no longer make excuses for things that shaped our lives. We instead embrace those things.

* Remember the fat mound of clay.

Everyone has it within his power to say, 'This I am today; that I will be tomorrow.'

My early life shaped me into this mound of clay. I can now choose to continue to be a mound of clay or I can choose to be a beautiful vase. Or a powerful sculpture. Or a giant castle. I have really stretched this clay analogy.

MY
[TYPICAL]
REACTIONS

In Sam Bracken's book, *My Orange Duffel Bag*, he shares the story of writing his personal inventory. We have taken that inspiration, and expanded it here. If we are going to take personal responsibility for lives, we must be brutally honest with ourselves. Often, we start with goals and dreams. We will get there. But first, let's determine where we are right now.

Fill out the personal inventory on the following pages to see who you are right now. What lump of clay are you currently? Each area has room for your personal interpretation, so feel free to answer according to those interpretations. For example, mental may be your emotional health; personal growth might be reading; spiritual may be in regards to your belief system or wholeness. Let's get started! Later in the book we will talk about how to become the person you desire to become... but right now we are going to focus on level one:

TAKING
PERSONAL
RESPONSIBILITY

PHYSICAL

Rate where you are on a scale of 1-100: 1 10 20 30 40 50 60 70 80 90 100

List your assets & liabilities:

_____   _____

_____   _____

Describe where you are right now in this area. Are you where you thought you'd be?

_____

_____

What has gone right? What has gone wrong?

_____

_____

Where would you like to be? When?

_____

_____

FAMILY

Rate where you are on a scale of 1-100: 1 10 20 30 40 50 60 70 80 90 100

List your assets & liabilities:

_____   _____

_____   _____

Describe where you are right now in this area. Are you where you thought you'd be?

_____

_____

What has gone right? What has gone wrong?

_____

_____

Where would you like to be? When?

_____

_____

MENTAL

Rate where you are on a scale of 1-100: 1 10 20 30 40 50 60 70 80 90 100

List your assets & liabilities:

_____   _____

_____   _____

Describe where you are right now in this area. Are you where you thought you'd be?

_____

_____

What has gone right? What has gone wrong?

_____

_____

Where would you like to be? When?

_____

_____

SPIRITUAL

Rate where you are on a scale of 1-100: 1 10 20 30 40 50 60 70 80 90 100

List your assets & liabilities:

_____   _____

_____   _____

Describe where you are right now in this area. Are you where you thought you'd be?

_____

_____

What has gone right? What has gone wrong?

_____

_____

Where would you like to be? When?

_____

_____

FINANCIAL

Rate where you are on a scale of 1-100:

1 10 20 30 40 50 60 70 80 90 100

List your assets & liabilities:

_____   _____

_____   _____

Describe where you are right now in this area. Are you where you thought you'd be?

_____

_____

What has gone right? What has gone wrong?

_____

_____

Where would you like to be? When?

_____

_____

CAREER / EDUCATIONAL

Rate where you are on a scale of 1-100:

1 10 20 30 40 50 60 70 80 90 100

List your assets & liabilities:

_____   _____

_____   _____

Describe where you are right now in this area. Are you where you thought you'd be?

_____

_____

What has gone right? What has gone wrong?

_____

_____

Where would you like to be? When?

_____

_____

Alright, you have completed steps one and two of taking personal responsibility so you can *Live Your List*. Now is where hard work comes into the picture. Step one of personal responsibility is taking ownership of your reactions. Step two is choosing your desired reactions. Step three is to actually react in your desired manner. Let's look at the last line of that Louis L'Amour quote:

The wish, however, must be implemented by deeds.

You will never turn from the big fat mound of clay into the masterpiece you are destined to be without hard work.*

Many of us have been told our whole life that we can do whatever we want in life! The world is our oyster! You can pursue any dream and become the person you want to be in life! You can even be president! Exclamation point for added effect!

Let me be the first to tell you that I agree with the above sentiment. I really do think you can take on the world and become the person you are destined to be. However, I think we have forgotten the most important part of the "you can do it" mantra:

You can be whoever you want to be and change the world...but it is going to require a ridiculous amount of hard work.

It will take hours and hours of intentionality and practice to make it a reality. Same can be said for most great things in life.

Hard work is not always fun. To be completely honest, this is an area in which I have consistently struggled. I like to do fun things.

* You thought I was done with the clay metaphor.

SLEEP ⟶ FUN

WATCH TV ⟶ FUN

HANG OUT WITH FRIENDS ⟶ FUN

TAKE PERSONAL RESPONSIBILITY ⟿ NOT FUN

WORK HARD ⟿ NOT FUN

I have always enjoyed charts that help me display my point. So I created the fun / not fun and easy / not easy chart.

	FUN	**NOT FUN**
EASY	Things that you are really good at and enjoy doing.	Things that you are really good at, but don't enjoy doing.
NOT EASY	Things that are not easy for you, but you really enjoy doing! These are typically challenging.	Things that you are not good at and don't enjoy doing.

We will typically do anything in the first quadrant! Why wouldn't we? These are things that we love to do and come naturally to us. They are easy and fun and we find an incredible amount of fulfillment while doing them.

If it is easy but not fun, we typically delay these tasks. These are things like filing paperwork, cleaning, organizing, etc.* If we want to accomplish these tasks we have to bear down and just get them done...eventually.

Most of us like doing things that are fun but not easy. These are the things that challenge us in a good way. It might be a new video game, playing a sport, or learning a new task at work. Of course hard work is involved, but it is fun so we don't mind.

The last quadrant is the one I want to focus on the most. These are the tasks that we do not enjoy and are not easy. It is learning new skills that we struggle with. It is trying to improve without seeing results. For me, it's eating healthy and running long distances. It's meditating, being quiet, being organized beyond necessity, and having hard conversations. It is also asking for forgiveness for my actions and forgiving those who have wronged me.

---

* Of course, some people find these tasks fun. If that is you then refer back to quadrant one and quit trying to organize the rest of us.

If I wanted to take true personal responsibility, I had to recognize my faults, pick the right actions to change, and then actually change by doing things that I am not good at and are not usually fun. For me, it's waking up early, it's being patient when i'm frustrated, it's remaining calm amidst chaos, and showing empathy to those who are hurting. It is also only eating three donuts instead of one, when I really should have zero.

It took me a long time to actually make this change and I had to learn how to take personal responsibility the hard way. This brings me to the next part of my *Live Your List* journey - the time I didn't take personal responsibility and it cost me **$25,000.**

THE
$25,000
LESSON

Life with sisters practically the same age as me was tough, but I made it. Actually, I made it with flying colors. I grew up to be by far the tallest person in my house. My mom is 5'7" and my dad is 5'7" and three quarters. Any time someone asked my dad how tall he was he said he was three quarters taller than my mom. My guess is that he was literally talking about quarters, and that if you stacked three on top of mom's head, she would be my dad's height.

My sisters ended up looking nothing like me. Both are around 5'4" and right over 100 pounds with small frames, blonde hair, fair skin, and light eyes. I ended up being tall, dark, and handsome, which translates to long, lanky, and well...handsome. I always said I was the chimney on our family photos. All of my family made a perfect line in a picture, and I was the tall, weird one on the end.

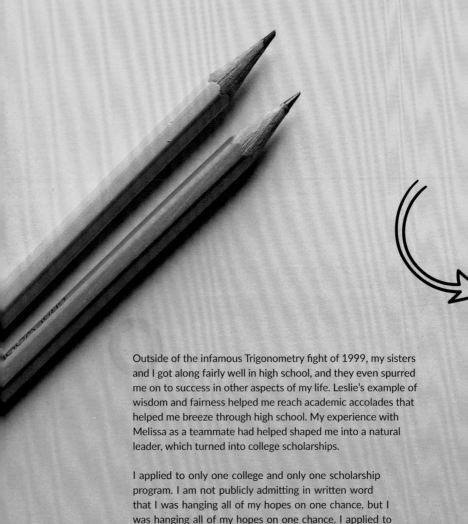

THE $25,000 LESSON

Outside of the infamous Trigonometry fight of 1999, my sisters and I got along fairly well in high school, and they even spurred me on to success in other aspects of my life. Leslie's example of wisdom and fairness helped me reach academic accolades that helped me breeze through high school. My experience with Melissa as a teammate had helped shaped me into a natural leader, which turned into college scholarships.

I applied to only one college and only one scholarship program. I am not publicly admitting in written word that I was hanging all of my hopes on one chance, but I was hanging all of my hopes on one chance. I applied to Northeastern State University and their President's Leadership Scholarship Program.

It was practically a full ride to a college that met all of my higher education requirements:

- ☑ Close to home, but far enough away I wouldn't have to see my parents every day.

- ☑ Co-ed. I was not going to a college with all males. No way, no how.

- ☑ Small enough of a campus that I could see anyone I wanted to see on any given day, but large enough to avoid all of the ladies I failed to romance.

- ☑ Cable television and high-speed Internet in the room. Outside of an extended stay in a hospital I had never had more than four channels at my place of residence. We had dial-up Internet at home, and if my sisters got a phone call while I was trying to download a song, I had to start completely over.

THAT WAS MY ENTIRE LIST.

I WAS NOT PICKY AND I HAD ALMOST
NO EXPECTATIONS.

Fortunately for me, after a lengthy application and interview process I got the scholarship. My guess is that they picked me because they needed more attractive males at the school. I didn't like that they used me to fill their attractive-male quota, but every person has their struggles so I took personal responsibility for my beauty and went to NSU after high school.

The first couple years were awesome. I joined a fraternity, met thousands of new people, got plugged into leadership roles across campus, and even met a few ladies. I was living the college lifestyle! I was like the guys from Animal House, except I didn't go to class as often as they did.

I found out that going to class was a very important part of the college experience. Surprisingly, professors expected you to show up and participate in the classes that the university was paying for me to attend. Going to class was not fun and it was not easy - it required hard work.

I had decided to major in biology as a pre-physical therapy student, and those science professors were the worst! They made their students "work" for an A. I mean, in high school the teachers gave me A's just so they didn't have to deal with me in their class. I actually had teachers ask me to leave class just to get me to stop talking.

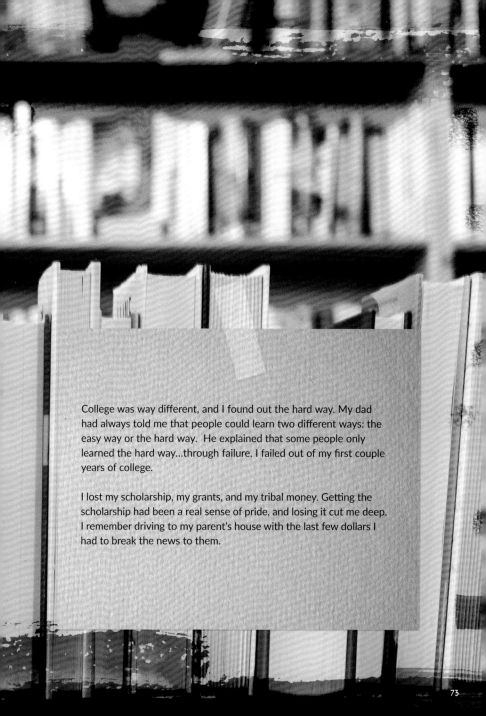

College was way different, and I found out the hard way. My dad had always told me that people could learn two different ways: the easy way or the hard way. He explained that some people only learned the hard way...through failure. I failed out of my first couple years of college.

I lost my scholarship, my grants, and my tribal money. Getting the scholarship had been a real sense of pride, and losing it cut me deep. I remember driving to my parent's house with the last few dollars I had to break the news to them.

It was a nerve-racking drive home. My parent's had been awfully proud of me. They were proud of all three of their kids. Melissa had been so influential that she got Bill Gates to pay for all of schooling at a private Christian school in Texas.[*] Leslie had gotten a full-ride to the University of Oklahoma and had even spent a semester in Japan.

Our driveway was almost a half-mile long, and I can remember how disappointed I was as I pulled up to my house. Dad greeted me outside and gave me a big hug. He was always so happy to see me, this was just going to make it worse. I asked him to get mom because I had to tell them some bad news.

---

[*] Turns out Uncle Bill paid for all 10 years of her education, and she walked across the stage with her Ph.D. and no debt.

I told them through big tears that I had lost it all. Everything I had worked for was gone. I asked them what I should do, and how I should get there. My mom was clearly upset, but she was trying hard to not make me feel worse.

I will always remember how the rest of the conversation went, because it was influential in changing the direction of the rest of my life. Dad looked me square in the eye and said,

"Son, we would love to help you get out of this mess, and we will always be there for you, but

YOU ARE 100% RESPONSIBLE FOR THIS,

and you will have to find your way out."

I got so mad at my parents. I told them that I had friends whose parents paid for their school. I told them that they should be proud of all of my other accomplishments. I had excelled on campus outside of the classroom, and I was gaining invaluable knowledge about how to interact with others. I told them that they should be paying for my school because that's what good parents do!

I know that conversation was hard for them, but they stuck to their guns. Mom and Dad had always taught me that it was up to me if I was going to be successful. Other people could influence me towards success, but I was the only one who could ultimately get me there.

I was basically starting from scratch. I had no money, no real job, and no real plan for the future. On that long drive back to college I made up my mind to prove to everyone that I could be responsible for my actions, that I would become the man that everyone expected me to become.

I bootstrapped it for the next couple years. I worked two or three jobs while retaking the classes I had failed. I put an emphasis on my education and worked hard to find a major that fit my personality and career ambitions. I took extra hours, studied late into the evening, and surrounded myself with others who were doing great work.

I took ownership of my actions, both positive and negative, to determine my outcome. I found that if my reaction to an event in my life was positive and I worked hard to correct it I typically had a positive outcome. If I got mad and frustrated at an event in my life my outcome was generally negative.

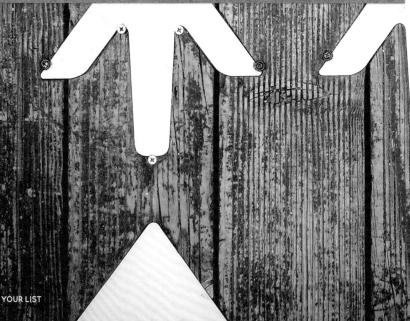

I started hustling toward my goals with renewed vigor and determination. I wasn't perfect, and I still made tons of mistakes. It was college, everyone makes tons of mistakes, but the difference this time was that I learned from my mistakes instead of getting upset.

It was these formative years in college that I focused on intentionally living my life and pointing into the direction I wanted it to go. I had spent so much time blaming others for my faults, and the entire time I should have been focusing on improving myself.

Eventually I was rewarded for my hustle and determination. Most importantly I got a new lease on my life. My friends and family noticed a change in my personality and enjoyed hanging out with me again. My sisters even cut back on their mind games because I handled them with incessant positivity.

It was during my last year of college that I had finally started to change from the fat mound of clay into the person I would later become. I was willing to take on the tasks that were not fun and not easy because I knew they were necessary to my future success. I had taken responsibility for my upbringing and realized my future was in my hands.

If you want to *Live Your List* you must take personal responsibility, but we all know that isn't enough. It is the place to start and the foundation for success, but with personal responsibility alone we are still just a mound of clay. We are now in control of who is shaping us, but it isn't until we start designing our future that we will eventually change shape.

In my last semester of college,

I DID JUST THAT.

live
YOUR
list

CREATE
LISTS

* You really thought I would stop with the clay analogy.

The best decision I made during my college redemption story was picking the correct college major for me. The year was 2004 and I wasn't nearly as old as I am now. I was a junior in college and editor of the school's newspaper, a position that came with tons of power and responsibility. Actually, it came with little responsibility and no power, but an unlimited supply of pizza, so I signed up for the job.

I had become a journalism major after my failed attempt at majoring in pre-physical therapy. No one had told me that becoming a physical therapist required zoology, a class I made a D in not once, but twice. It is hard to focus on animal genetics when there were girls around, and college had lots of girls. The science department had very few. After having the serious conversation with my parents about taking responsibility for my actions, I decided I needed a new major, and fast.

The communications department had a sign over the door that read, "Not doing well in science? Become a Mass Communications major!" It didn't actually have that sign, but it might as well have. I started taking mass comm classes and thoroughly enjoyed talking in front of groups and writing papers that weren't about Novel Cell Surface Anchoring Mechanism of Prokaryotic Secreted Protein.

[CREATE LISTS]

After a year of entry-level journalism classes, I wrote for the newspaper and eventually became editor. Our adviser was Dr. Eversole, a wonderful professor and mentor who preferred to be called Dana. Dana loved empowering her students and giving them opportunities to be awesome, so she sent me to New York City to a conference at the *New York Times*.

I had traveled some as a teen, but I had never been to the Big Apple. I certainly had never traveled this far by myself. Dana was brave. She put me in charge of a couple hundred dollars and sent me off to NYC without an agenda or itinerary. All I knew was that I had to be at the *New York Times* at 8 am on Monday. Everything else was up to me.

My time in NYC was a whirlwind. I had less than three days to attend a conference, see the sights, and hopefully get back on the plane to come home. I only got a few hours of sleep as I spent every hour available touring the massive city. I do not remember much from the conference, but I have a few experiences from that trip embedded into my memory.

1. After being there for less than 15 minutes, I was asked to buy weed. I think they could smell the tourist exuding off of my bewildered look.

2. I did not have enough money to place a deposit for a hotel room. Which was a problem because I like beds as opposed to sidewalks.

3. No one told me the subway system or Central Park was scary after dark. I found this out quickly.

4. The massive space left from the World Trade Towers was more than I could handle. Everything in this city went straight up, except for this spot, which went down.

5. Just because the kabobs on the street smell good does not mean they taste good.

6. Being a small-town tourist who takes the wrong bus and ends up in Harlem with a bunch of luggage in tow makes me pee myself a little.

The thing I remember most about the trip, the thing that changed my life forever was the plane ride home.

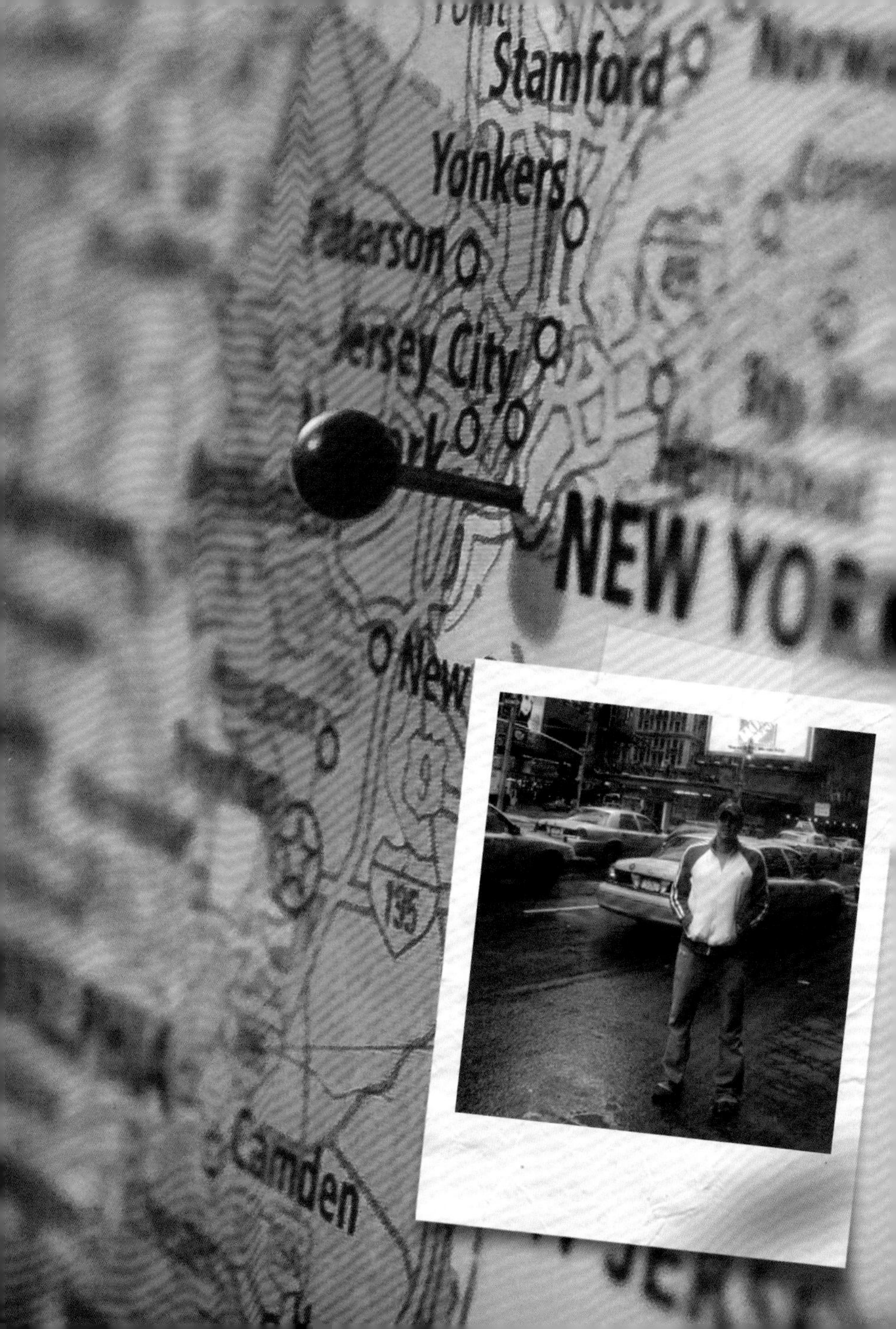
Stamford
Yonkers
Paterson
Jersey City
NEW YOR
Camden

[CREATE LISTS]

I was safe and secure on the flight and feeling sleepy from my experiences, but I couldn't drift to sleep on the plane. It might have been because of my excitement from the trip, but mostly it was because of the 400-pound woman snoring next to me. She took up her seat and half of mine, and every snore sounded like a tractor starting.

I took out my journalist notepad that the *New York Times* gave me, and started scribbling notes about my trip. I was a journalist for crying out loud! I needed to write!

I wrote about my experience on top of the Empire State Building. About how I had never felt so small and insignificant as I did while look out on the skyline of the city. I wrote about walking around the financial district and seeing the hustle and bustle of people way more important than me. I wrote about seeing the Statue of Liberty, something I had always wanted to see, and never thought I would be able to.

It was from this time of honing my skills as a reporter that inspiration struck. I had seen so many amazing things, so I needed to create a list of awesome things I had done to record it all. I looked back at my trip and even back at my life and starting jotting down things the highlights of my young life.

After two minutes I had created my very short list and was not inspired any longer. How had I been so busy for the first 21 years of my life, but not really done anything? How had I squandered my opportunities to impact others and change lives? I asked myself a question that many of us ask in times like this:

HOW DID I GET HERE?

I decided at that moment that my life would change. I would stop being mundane and start being intentional. From here on out I would do the things I had always wanted to do, but had been too busy or lazy to accomplish. Right then and there, next to the 400-pounder, I created a list of things I wanted to accomplish before I died.

Many of you have heard about this concept. It is most commonly known as a Bucket List, and there was even a movie about a couple of rich old dudes checking things off their list when they found out they were about to die.

I didn't want to wait that long.

I wanted to start working on my list while I was on the plane. I wanted to start accomplish things while I was young, so when I was old and rich I could tell my grandchildren* the stories of my awesomeness.

Feeling excited, I started my list. Like most Bucket Lists, I started with travel destinations. I wanted to go to Antarctica, the pyramids, and make a guard laugh at Buckingham Palace. I wanted to visit all 50 US states and kiss on top of the Eiffel Tower.

This really fired me up, and I began to think of all of the adventures I wanted to pursue. I wanted to climb Mt. Everest and take an African safari. I wanted to bungee jump, skydive, and scuba dive.

I started dreaming about my life goals and career ambitions. I certainly wanted to graduate college and eventually write a book (Boom! I am literally doing this right now). I wanted to start my own business and speak to crowds of thousands of people.

* Or random strangers... let's be honest, it will be both.

I thought about personal and family goals that I had always wanted. I wanted to get in shape and have six-pack abs. I wanted to run a marathon and maybe even an Ironman triathlon. I wanted to be married someday and have kids. I dreamed of having a relationship with my grandchildren that was as awesome as I had with my Grandpa.

I continued to add things to my list until it was about 75 buckets* in length. How could I achieve all of these things? I was young, inexperienced, poor, and not very talented. I had no fame or rich uncles who could support this venture.

I didn't know those answers then, but I knew I was going to find out. I was determined, inspired, and a little annoyed by the snoring from the lady next to me. I put up my awesome *NY Times* notepad and shut my eyes. I dreamed about how awesome my life was going to be, and how I was going to achieve it.

* Items on a Bucket List.

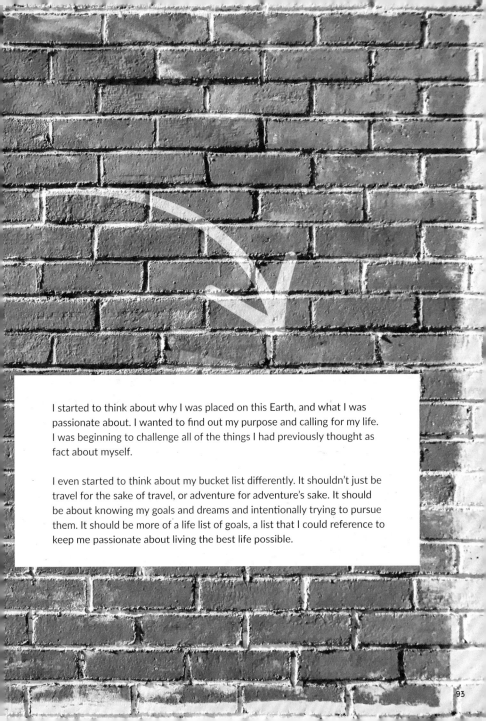

I started to think about why I was placed on this Earth, and what I was passionate about. I wanted to find out my purpose and calling for my life. I was beginning to challenge all of the things I had previously thought as fact about myself.

I even started to think about my bucket list differently. It shouldn't just be travel for the sake of travel, or adventure for adventure's sake. It should be about knowing my goals and dreams and intentionally trying to pursue them. It should be more of a life list of goals, a list that I could reference to keep me passionate about living the best life possible.

I hoped my bucket list would challenge me to be intentional about the decisions I made for my future. I hoped it could help me find a career that was perfect for my calling in life, even though I had no idea what that calling was yet. My bucket list included all of the things I wanted to see, do, experience, and even accomplish in my life.

I knew that when I returned from New York City and resumed my life back in Oklahoma that things would be different, and it was! All of the hard work and focus on intentionality paid off, and in my fifth year of college* I was accepted back into the leadership scholarship and received all of my grants and tribal funds. I eventually graduated with honors and was selected as the Outstanding Male Senior for the entire University.

* I always told people I was redshirted academically.

My college career kicked off a journey towards a *Live Your List* lifestyle. A journey of taking responsibility for my actions through a positive mentality. A journey of pursuing the things that I had always dreamed for my life.

VIEW RYAN'S
BUCKET LIST
(AS OF NOVEMBER 2017)

#	ITEM	COMPLETE	ACHIEVEMENT DATE
1	Set Foot on North America, South America, Asia, Europe, Australia, Antartica and Africa		
2	Ride in a Hot Air Balloon	X	7/8/2007
3	Personally Know Someone Famous	X	5/25/2005
4	Dance with Miss America	X	3/5/2005
5	Swim with a Dolphin	X	3/18/2008
6	Learn a Foreign Language and Actually Use It		
7	Have my Portrait Painted	X	12/23/2010
8	Watch a Space Shuttle Launch		
9	Be an Extra in a Film		
10	Skydive	X	3/15/2015
11	Scuba Dive		
12	Ride a Train	X	6/9/2007
13	Be a Member of a Studio Audience		
14	Send a Message in a Bottle and get a Response		
15	Go to Space		
16	Plant a Tree and Watch it Grow	X	4/22/2010
17	Learn to Ballroom Dance...Properly		
18	Sit on a Jury		
19	Write an Autobiography		
20	Be Someone's Mentor		
21	Shower in a Waterfall	X	11/12/2012
22	Learn to Legitimately Play a Song on any Musical Instrument		
23	Teach someone illiterate to read		
24	Spend the night in a haunted place	X	2/24/2012
25	See a Lunar Eclipse	X	3/3/2007
26	Spend New Year's Eve in Times Square		
27	Drive Across America Coast-to-Coast		
28	Go Snow Skiing	X	3/14/2007
29	Crash an extravagant wedding		
30	Write my will	X	6/10/2014
31	Sleep under the stars	X	6/5/2012
32	Go white-water rafting	X	7/24/2010

#	ITEM	COMPLETE	ACHIEVEMENT DATE
33	Own my own house	X	4/13/2009
34	Grow a garden and eat the produce	X	7/15/2015
35	Have six-pack abs		
36	Go Deep Sea Fishing		
37	Spend time at a concentration camp		
38	Create a Family Tree		
39	Spoil my grandchildren		
40	Catch a foul ball or home-run at a MLB game		
41	Hit a hole-in-one		
42	Run a marathon	X	4/26/2009
43	Swim with sharks		
44	Experience weightlessness – no gravity		
45	Go to a sumo wrestling match		
46	See a tornado touch ground	X	4/29/2016
47	Go to an active volcano		
48	Go to a nudist colony		
49	Travel on a safari	X	10/18/2017
50	Ride a bull		
51	Run with the bulls in Pamplona		
52	Attend a Jewish wedding		
53	Go to a Pow-Wow		
54	Ride a cable car in San Francisco	X	7/19/2017
55	Watch the Yankees-Red Sox in Fenway Park and Yankee Stadium		
56	Try to make a guard laugh at Buckingham Palace	X	12/29/2012
57	Walk a length of the Great Wall of China	X	10/23/2010
58	Go to a drive-in movie theater		
59	See Mt. Rushmore	X	8/4/2012
60	Drive an 18-wheeler		
61	Eat a meal from a world class chef		
62	Crash a Hollywood Studio		
63	Meet someone famous randomly		
64	Spend a day in a spa	X	3/17/2008
65	Walk the red carpet at a huge event		

#	ITEM	COMPLETE	ACHIEVEMENT DATE
66	Stay at a 5-star hotel		
67	See Stonehenge	X	12/30/2012
68	Stand next to a pyramid		
69	Ride a Gondola in Venice		
70	Take a yoga class	X	6/28/2011
71	Take a photography class	X	7/1/2005
72	Shake hands with a President		
73	Learn how to sail		
74	See the Northern Lights		
75	Kiss on top the Eiffel Tower	X	1/1/2013
76	Learn to Juggle	X	7/9/2008
77	Get a tattoo	X	3/9/2008
78	Crowd Surf at a rock concert		
79	Bungy Jump		
80	Save someone's life		
81	Get a book published		
82	Get a standing ovation		
83	Kill a wild game animal	X	12/24/2009
84	Make a clay pot		
85	Relax in Tahiti for at least two weeks		
86	Live abroad		
87	Eat frog legs and gumbo and shrimp in the Deep South	X	11/27/2008
88	Snowboard		
89	Be on a game show	X	9/18/2012
90	Go treasure hunting		
91	Be involved in a heist		
92	Own a pet monkey		
93	Land a flip on a wakeboard		
94	Surf the waves in Hawaii		
95	Enter a professional Ping-Pong tournament		
96	Give my daughter away at her wedding to a man who deserves her		
97	Watch the sunset on a beach on my honeymoon	X	3/19/2008
98	Coach my son's little league team		

#	ITEM	COMPLETE	ACHIEVEMENT DATE
99	Run my own successful business (1 million in one year)	X	11/21/2017
100	Watch OU-Texas at the Red River Rivalry	X	10/11/2008
101	Walk across hot coals		
102	Go to all 50 U.S. States	X	10/14/2016
103	Be on a Reality TV show		
104	Be completely out of debt		
105	Go on a cruise	X	7/11/2013
106	Drive through a Redwood Tree		
107	Ride the Skycoaster at the Royal Gorge	X	6/24/2010
108	Go to the Summer Olympic Games with my Dad		
109	Have acupuncture		
110	Visit the Hoover Dam	X	6/15/2013
111	Climb Chichen Itza	X	11/8/2017
112	Stand beside the Christ the Redeemer statue	X	6/21/2012
113	Walk around the Colosseum in Rome	X	1/2/2013
114	Hang out with a Llama at Machu Picchu	X	11/25/2016
115	Explore Petra		
116	Take a picture in front of the Taj Mahal		
117	Go to Dusseldorf, Germany and tour Eller Castle		
118	Travel to the center of all religion, Jerusalem		
119	Ride a Segway		
120	Attend a World Cup Match		
121	Go Ice Fishing		
122	Take the Polar Plunge in a cold weather country	X	7/27/2015
123	Give a commencement speech		
124	Sleep on a Trampoline	X	6/5/2012
125	Swim in every ocean		
126	Fly an airplane	X	5/28/2013
127	Go to a NASCAR race		
128	Have a street named after me		
129	Tour the White House		
130	Set a World Record		
131	Get something patented		

#	ITEM	COMPLETE	ACHIEVEMENT DATE
132	Catch a trout while fly fishing with Stephen and Josh		
133	Eat at a Brazilian Steakhouse in Brazil	X	6/21/2012
134	Visit an orphanage in a foreign country	X	6/22/2012
135	Ride a Double Decker Bus in London	X	12/29/2012
136	Sit atop the London Eye	X	12/29/2012
137	Give a TED Talk	X	9/23/2014
138	Stand upon a glacier	X	10/9/2014
139	Go to the North Pole		
140	Go to the South Pole		
141	Jump off a waterfall.		
142	Go paragliding in a foreign country		
143	Take the walk of faith at Tienanmen Mountain in China		
144	Travel to an international city after throwing a dart at a map		
145	Climb to the base of Mount Everest		
146	Take a round-the-world cruise		
147	Swim in the Devil's Pool at Victoria Falls.	X	10/18/2017
148	Drive a professional race car.		
149	Visit every country in the world.		
150	Visit every county in Oklahoma		
151	Camp in every US National Park		
152	Camp in every OK State Park		
153	Attend the Super Bowl		
154	Go to Final Four Game		
155	Watch the OKC Thunder in the NBA Finals		
156	Travel in an RV with Kristin for a summer		
157	Take my family on a car family vacation		
158	Step Foot in Every Country in North America		
159	Step Foot in Every Country in South America		
160	Step Foot in Every Country in the Americas		
161	Step Foot in Every Country in Europe		
162	Step Foot in Every Country in Africa		
163	Step Foot in Every Country in Asia		
164	Step Foot in Every Country in Oceana		

#	ITEM	COMPLETE	ACHIEVEMENT DATE
165	Travel through every US county		
166	Be married for the rest of my life		
167	Graduate with a doctorate degree		
168	Write a book with My Mom		
169	Attend a professional seminar with Melissa		
170	Take a trip with Leslie		
171	Take my family to Disney World	X	4/22/2017
172	Complete a Half-Ironman Competition	X	9/24/2012
173	Complete a Full Ironman Competition		
174	Hike for a week on the Appalachian Trail		
175	Drive a boat		
176	Go on a whale-watching tour		
177	Have a Scholarship Foundation in my Name		
178	Spend the night in a jail cell		
179	Pay for someone's college education (other than my children)		
180	Spend time in a sensory deprivation tank		
181	Walk with lions in their natural habitat	X	10/16/2017
182	Ride a camel in the middle east	X	10/12/2017
183	Experience a Total Solar Eclipse	X	8/21/2017
184	Eat a traditional meal in the Middle East	X	10/12/2017
185	Soak in the mist of Niagra Falls	X	10/15/2016
186	Watch someone become a US citizen	X	5/23/2017
187	Ride an Elephant	X	10/16/2017
188	Walk across the Capilano Suspension Bridge	X	12/20/2013
189	Stand Next to Seljalandsfoss in Iceland	X	
190	Work with a school in Africa	X	10/17/2017
191	Ski in the Mall in Dubai	X	
192	Practice Kung Fu in the Shaolin Temple	X	
193	Hang out on top of the St. Louis Arch	X	
194	Walk out on the Skybox at the Sears Tower	X	
195	Hang out with Koalas in Australia	X	
196	Try every flavor of Snow Cone at the local snow cone stand	X	
197	Graduate with a Master's Degree	X	

#	ITEM	COMPLETE	ACHIEVEMENT DATE
198	Defend the Alamo	X	
199	Freeze in a Cryotherapy Tube	X	10/10/2017
200	Air Boat across an Alligator Infested Swamp		
201	Arrive By Seaplane to a remote location		
202	Attempt to ice climb over a glacier		
203	Bamboo raft down a mystical river		
204	Be a seat filler at the Oscars		
205	Bet on a horse at the horse races		
206	Bury a time capsule and open it years later		
207	Explore a cave while spelunking		
208	Go to a ceremony of a religion that is not your own		
209	Karate chop and break a board		
210	Plant a flag on top of a mountain		
211	Rise above the water while Flyboarding in a Water Jet Pack		
212	Stand up paddle board		
213	Team up with someone and ride a tandem bicycle		
214	Walk on stilts		
215	Figure out how many licks it actually takes to get to the tootsie roll center of a Tootsie Pop		
216	Perform stand up comedy at a comedy club		
217	Solve a Rubik's cube without cheating		
218	Celebrate my 50th Wedding Anniversary with the love of my life		
219	Attend the NBA All-Star Game		
220	Summit Mount Kilimanjaro in Tanzania		
221	Guess the age of a Baobab Tree in Madagascar		
222	Watch the Migration of the Animals at Serengeti in Tanzania		
223	Attempt to ride a train in India		
224	Admire the Shwedagon Pagoda in Rangoon, Burma		
225	Behold Bagan in Myanmar		
226	Brave the climb to the Tiger's Nest, Taktsang Palphug		
227	Cruise in Ha Long Bay, Vietnam		
228	Experience Istanbul's Call to Prayer		

#	ITEM	COMPLETE	ACHIEVEMENT DATE
229	Face the Lion's Rock at the ancient royal compound of Sigiriya in Sri Lanka		
230	Feel the awe of history in the Buddhist cave temples of Dambulla		
231	Find myseflf lost in a crowd in Tokyo		
232	Float in the Dead Sea		
233	Go vertical caving in Yogyakarta, Indonesia		
234	Hike the Caucasus in Georgia		
235	Hold on for dear life at the Walk of Faith in Tianmen Mountain		
236	Hunt with eagles in Mongolia		
237	Participate in the color festival (Holi) in India		
238	Ride the elevator to top of the Burj Khalifa in Dubai		
239	Chase waterfalls in Bosnia-Herzegovina		
240	Climb Leukerbad Via Ferrata in Switzerland		
241	Climb Skellig Islands off of the coast of Ireland		
242	Cross the Straits of Gibraltar on a ferry		
243	Drive as fast as I can on the Autobahn in Germany		
244	Touch the white walls of Santorini		
245	Walk through the Plitvice Lakes in Croatia		
246	Bike down Haleakala in Hawaii		
247	Board down an active volcano in Nicaragua		
248	Commit to doing the Half-Dome ascent in Yosemite National Park		
249	Catch mist at Angel Falls in Venezuela		
250	Reflect at Salar de Uyuni in Bolivia		
251	Swing at the end of the world in Ecuador		
252	Unexpectedly discover Kaieteur Falls, Guyana		
253	Jump off of a cliff into a Cenote	X	11/8/2017
254	Unexpectedly discover Kaieteur Falls, Guyana		

I don't care what phase of life you are in right now, I want you to start your journey, too. On the next few pages, we will walk you through the steps necessary to create your list of life goals and dreams by writing out some buckets.

[CREATE LISTS]

If you already have a list, then add some new ones. If you have a list and haven't written it down, then you have bucket thoughts and not a bucket list. Write it down. **Be creative and fun. Be specific. Do some research.**

In the back of the book, you will find a list of 1,001 bucket list items. Steal them if you need to! Just make sure to follow the Ten Commandments of bucket lists:

BUCKET LIST
TEN COMMANDMENTS

1 Thou Shalt Write Thy Bucket List Down

2 It Shalt Contain Anything Thou Wants To Accomplish Before Death

3 Thou Shalt Talk About Thy List With Thy Family and Thy Close Friends and Thy Strangers

4 Thou Shalt Not Add Buckets Which Holdeth No Meaning

5 Thou Shalt Review Thy List Regularly

6 Thou Shalt Feel No Guilt For Stealing One's Idea

7 Thou Shalt Feel No Anger For One Stealing Your Idea

8 Thou Shalt Research Thy Buckets

9 Thou Shalt Celebrate Thou Successes

10 Thou Shalt Never Compare Lists Lest You Be Given To Pride Or Inferiority

Follow these commandments as you write your list.

BUCKET LIST BY 5s

5 TRAVEL LIST BUCKET ITEMS

5 ADVENTURE BUCKET LIST ITEMS

5 THINGS YOU WANT TO LEARN

5 FAMILY
BUCKET LIST ITEMS

5 EDUCATIONAL BUCKET LIST ITEMS

5 CAREER
BUCKET LIST ITEMS

I want to see your bucket lists! Share pictures, or some of the buckets you are most excited about by tweeting me (*@ryan_eller*), posting on Instagram with the hashtag *#LiveYourList*, or join our Facebook group at *facebook.com/groups/liveyourlist*.

live
• YOUR
list

Write something awesome.

It is important to remember that the *Live Your List* levels are sequential and build off of each other. You cannot start to pursue your dreams and goals without taking personal responsibility of your life. You can also not start living your life to the fullest without honestly defining what those dreams and goals are for your life.

You see, every journey has a start, and some would even argue it is the most important part of the journey. However, I couldn't achieve these dreams and ambitions without direction. I needed to organize and plan my life so I could point it in the direction I wanted it to go. I needed goals, and I needed them fast. It took me getting fat and complacent for me to truly understand how to put a system in place to efficiently pursue my journey. It is great to have a list to pursue, but the list is not going to check itself. We must start to take those items and turn them into goals.

After I wrote my initial bucket list, I knew I needed to take action. I looked over my list and picked the hardest item to complete. The item that would not be fun or easy. Then I completely changed my life to make it a reality.

live
YOUR
list

WHAT'S
YOUR ID?

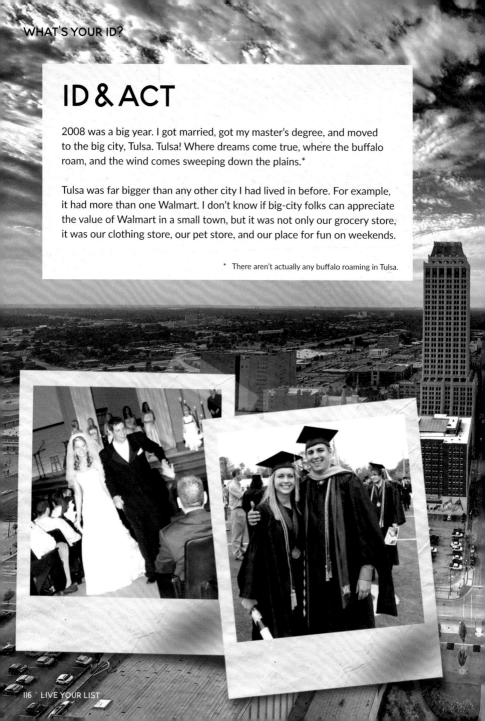

ID & ACT

2008 was a big year. I got married, got my master's degree, and moved to the big city, Tulsa. Tulsa! Where dreams come true, where the buffalo roam, and the wind comes sweeping down the plains.*

Tulsa was far bigger than any other city I had lived in before. For example, it had more than one Walmart. I don't know if big-city folks can appreciate the value of Walmart in a small town, but it was not only our grocery store, it was our clothing store, our pet store, and our place for fun on weekends.

* There aren't actually any buffalo roaming in Tulsa.

I kid you not, in high school and in college, if people got bored they went to Walmart. Conversations went like this:

> **Me: Hey, you doing anything tonight?**
>
> **Friend: No, what about you?**
>
> **Me: Nothing at all. I'm pretty bored. You know what might be fun? Going to Walmart!**
>
> **Friend: That is a great idea! We will see people we know there, and you never know what kind of random pets that people will be selling in the parking lot. That guy might be back trying to sell his baby emus.**
>
> **Me: Don't forget to mention that there is a great chance someone will get arrested while we are there! I'll see you in five minutes.**[*]

[*] It never took more than five minutes to get anywhere.

Tulsa photography by David Bouchard, @onebouchard

Tulsa had so many Walmarts I couldn't keep track! The only thing Tulsa had more than Walmarts were QuikTrip gas stations. I had always heard about the greatness of QuikTrip but never experienced it first-hand. My small towns had no QuikTrips, but people would come to our college town and talk about how much they missed a gas station.

I thought they were crazy. After all, most Walmarts had gas stations and Walmart was where it was at! They insisted that I wouldn't know until I lived in Tulsa, so the moment I moved there I checked it out for myself.

They were right to love QuikTrip. It was the Walmart of gas stations. They had the cheapest gas, the best drinks, and a donut selection that would rival any donut shop. If my excitement about Walmart and QuikTrip tell you anything, it tells you that I hadn't lived in a big town before 2008.

WHAT'S YOUR ID?

And 2008 was a big year because so many of the huge bucket list goals that I had been working towards were checked off of my list. I had been trying to get married for most of my life. I knew it was something I wanted to do, and it had finally happened. I got the master's degree that I would have never thought possible, and I had moved to a city with multiple Walmarts. Life was good.

However, anytime you achieve multiple life goals at one time it is easy to get stuck while trying to figure out what to do during your new phase of life. I had achieved some huge things, but I didn't know what I should do next. I had prepared for this moment, however, and I grabbed my bucket list. If I was stuck, the best thing to do was to try and do something on the ole' BL!

I decided I wanted to pick an item that was going to be very challenging for me, and something I didn't think I would ever be able to accomplish. I wanted an item that required a considerable amount of time and would give me a sense of accomplishment when completed.

I scoured my list and saw the item immediately. It almost leapt off of the page it was so perfect for me. I dismissed it because it was too hard. There was no way I could actually do this item. However, no matter how hard I tried to ignore it I couldn't keep from staring at this item...

#42 RUN A MARATHON

No way. I couldn't do that. I had spent too much time eating donuts from QuikTrip for me to be able to run 26.2 miles! Do you know how far that is? Go drive 26.2 miles in your car, you will think it takes forever. Now go try to run that far. That is insane.

Of all of the buckets on my list, this one scared me the most. Not because I wasn't a gifted athlete, but because I had never finished something that was challenging and because I had a unique talent of quitting things that were not fun. I didn't have the marathon mentality, and I knew it.

After much contemplation and encouragement from my wife, I decided to take up marathon training. It wasn't my first time running, but I was nervous. As long as I can remember, I have been a gifted runner. Not an elite runner, but pretty dang fast and it came very naturally to me.

122 · LIVE YOUR LIST

WHAT'S YOUR ID?

When I was about six years old, our church had a five-mile fun run/walk for missions that pretty much the whole church participated in. I ran the whole thing and finished in first place, far ahead of the other participants (it wasn't a serious run).*

I ran a mile for the President's Fitness Challenge in 5th grade and I distinctly remember running it in 6 minutes and 22 seconds. One classmate, Baby John Coker, was right there with me, and everyone else was at least a half mile behind. I would have been considered the most presidentially fit except I couldn't pass the stretching portion of the exam.

My freshman year of high school I found my best races, the 400 and the 800. I remember running my first 800 at the high school level, I hated it! It was a half mile of pure torture. Two laps of agony as I practically sprinted around the track.

I finished my first race in 2 minutes and 30 seconds. Not bad, but not great, and certainly not good enough to medal. I swore off the 800 and told my friends and family that I would never run the race again, and I didn't, until the next track meet when my coach made me run it again.

* It was a short-lived victory because the only thing anyone remembers from that run is that a bird pooped on my youth pastor's head.

The only time I really ran was in practice or at meets, and I didn't take practice seriously, mostly because my coach, the football coach, didn't take track seriously. Each race remained difficult, but I got faster and faster. At the regional meet I can remember looking behind me on the straight-away to see if anyone was going to catch me (very poor form), but no one ever did. I placed first that day and earned a trip to the state championship track meet...the only kid from my entire school to go to state in any sport that year.*

* We weren't known for athletic prowess.

As I lined up at the state track meet to run my race, I noticed that I was the only freshmen in the 800. There were also no sophomores. Only juniors and seniors and myself, the fresh-faced lanky 14-year-old. When the starting gun went off I raced full-steam ahead. My enthusiasm rushed straight through me as I jumped out to an early lead.

I ran a 52-second first lap, which would put me on pace for a national high school record, not just an Oklahoma state record. At the 500 meter mark I was at least 4-5 paces ahead of the entire group of older runners, but I was starting to struggle. At the 600 meter mark, I heard several coaches yell "GO!" and in a matter of seconds nine of the 13 other runners passed me at one time.

I tried my best to keep up, but my inexperience and lack of training had betrayed me, I just couldn't do it. I gutted it out and finished a respectable 7th overall. I finished my second lap in 66 seconds, 14 seconds slower than my first lap for a time of 1:59. This was some of the first lessons running taught me...it doesn't matter where you start, but where you finish, and you can only go so far on talent and ability, hard work will take you the rest of the way.

In the beginning of my sophomore year, in basketball offseason, Coach Daniels had us run timed 400s. He was going to work us out all offseason and re-time us at the end. I ran my 400 in 49 seconds, my fastest time ever.

I had not trained, had not practiced and was actually out of shape. I was just older and more physically mature so my times were great. That 49-second time was fast enough to win state in almost every class in any year, and certainly in my smaller division. I was ready to put in the effort to be a champion.

THEN EVERYTHING CHANGED.

A week later I was coming back home from my girlfriend's house with two friends. It was after midnight when we were hit head on. A drunk man passed out while driving and crashed into us going over 70 miles an hour, and he died on impact.

Our driver, Ryan Irvin, knew it was coming, but couldn't stop in time, and our truck was demolished. We were demolished too. Ryan had broken bones all throughout his face, a hole in his intestines, punctured lungs and a busted up heel. My best friend Brandon Nickell came out pretty much unscathed and he was extremely lucky (We told people he was in a bike wreck). I was not so fortunate.

I broke my left hip in 3 places, my pelvis in 7 places, my tailbone in 3 places, my nose and shattered my right leg. I spent the next 42 days in the hospital in traction and a cast from my toe to my hip. I got out of the hospital standing 6'2" and weighing 128 pounds, confined to a wheelchair and unable to walk. I even walked with a noticeable limp until I went to college.

The doctors and physical therapists said I would never run again, and even if I did it would never be competitive. I have forgotten more than I can remember from that time, but I do know it took rehab everyday for nearly a year to relearn how to walk and to run again. I transitioned from wheelchair to crutches to a cane.

I had to work harder than I had in my entire life just to do the things I took for granted in life.

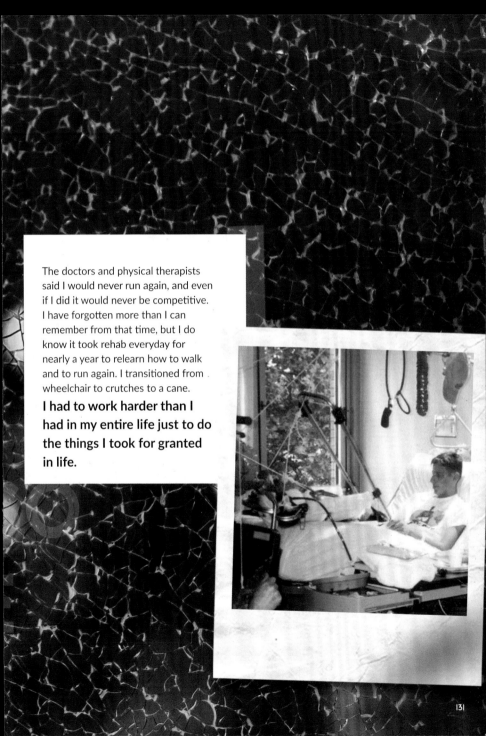

The wreck was in the end of August, I was released from the hospital in October, I was finally in crutches in November, a cane in February, and I ran track that April. It was the proudest day of my life. I only ran the 800, I limped around the track, I came in last, and I threw up after the race...but I could not have been happier. That was the second time running taught me a few lessons...

DON'T EVER LET ANYONE ELSE TELL YOU WHAT YOU CANNOT DO IN YOUR LIFE, AND NEVER, EVER GIVE UP.

Throughout the rest of high school I came nearly close to 100% recovered and tore my ACL, forcing me to forego all athletics my senior year. I missed running, but gave it up in college while I lived the fraternity life and ~~studied~~ slept through class.

Fast forward 10 years past the wreck. I was married and living in Tulsa, overweight with no friends in the new big city, and I decided I needed a challenge. This bucket list item was scary, but no scarier than relearning how to walk in 1998.

I knew that I couldn't achieve this without proper planning. If I was going to succeed and actually finish this race, I had to think of this as more than just an item on a list. It had to become a goal.

Running a marathon was the first bucket list item that became a serious goal for my life. Most of the buckets I had previously checked were small items, like learning how to yodel or traveling on a train. This one would take months if not years of consistent training to achieve.

IT WAS MY IMPOSSIBLE DREAM.

WHAT'S YOUR ID?

If you want to *Live Your List* it is utterly important to figure out your ID - your Impossible Dream. For it to be considered an impossible dream it must fit the following criteria:

It Makes You Pee a Little

If you are not nervous about being able to accomplish this goal then it is not an ID. You need to wonder if you are going to be able to accomplish the goal. You need to be scared that you won't actually achieve it even with hard work.

Makes You Wanna Cuss

Not literally curse. I am not encouraging cursing. This is a family book full of great stories with a handsome protagonist. However, Impossible Dreams might make you want to cuss. They will not be easy and you know it. They could potentially not be fun too and you are OK with that.

You Know You're Gonna Need Help

If you can achieve your ID without assistance than it is not a big enough dream. You will need help in some capacity - financially, emotionally, physically, or literally.

My ID was to run a marathon.
Let's see if it fits the Impossible Dream criteria:

It Makes You Pee a Little

When I set out to run a marathon I weighed over 240 pounds and my activity level was the same as a potato. I knew that I wasn't going to be able to accomplish this goal without losing weight and having the activity level of at least a potato rolling down a hill. Yes, I was nervous. I was scared I was going to fail. I was concerned I was going to quit like I had done most hard things in my life. It made me want to pee a little.

Make You Wanna Cuss

Full transparency here - I did cuss when I completed my first 22-mile training run. I didn't say the worst curse words, but I did cuss.* I had been slowly building up to the marathon distance, but 22 miles was six miles further than I had ever run. I was already having a bad day - it was hot, I was tired, and I felt like a potato. Then my running coach decided that at mile 22 we should run an extra half mile so I could experience torture.** After I hit 22 miles I got so mad that I sat down on the concrete and cursed. I was mad at everyone and everything. Looking back I know it was good for me to push myself. In the moment I didn't see it that way.

You Know You're Gonna Need Help

I knew I could not do this alone. You have already figured out that I got a coach. I also found a running group and sought advice from experienced runners. I listened and learned and researched. I could not do this one alone.

* Sorry mom.
** I'm not sure if that was her goal, but it worked.

137

So, running a marathon is my Impossible Dream. What is yours? **Write it down and make sure it fits the ID criteria.**

ACT

Marathoning was my ID. But how to do I actually complete a marathon?

You would think that the "how-to" on running a marathon would be a short list. It should go something like this:

1. Put one foot in front of the other.
2. Lean forward.
3. Instead of falling put your other foot forward.
4. Continue momentum to keep from falling.
5. Do this for 26.2 miles.

I thought running would be this easy. As mentioned above, I had run before. This was not my first rodeo. I bought some generic cross-training shoes from a department store, put on my basketball shorts and favorite T-shirt, and headed out of the door.

We were fortunate to live by the Arkansas River by downtown Tulsa, and it has beautiful running trails that stretch for over 25 miles throughout the city. Our apartments backed up to the trail, therefore finding a good place to run was easy for me.

When I made it to the trail, I acted liked I was stretching for the occasional jogger who passed. After all, I was pretty sure people stretched before they exercised. It had been so long that I couldn't remember. I didn't stretch before eating donuts, so I had gotten pretty rusty on the rules of exercise.

My goal for the day was to run one mile. That was it. I was pretty confident that I could go one mile without stopping, and I picked one mile because it seemed like a great starting place for my training.

I decided to start training for the marathon in the late afternoon in August, mostly because I am an idiot. Tulsa may not be the hottest place on Earth in August. Maybe it is somewhere in Iraq or along the equator. But if you are overweight and haven't run in several years, Tulsa in August might as well be the surface of the sun.

In the past, I had been a fast runner. Six-minute miles were nothing to me. I could do that running backwards.* When I hit the trail I started off at a fast pace. No reason not to get this mile over with as soon as possible. I found a flaw in my plan about 100 yards into the Tulsa heat. I had started too fast.

*Not literally. The world record for running a mile backwards is 5 minutes 54.25 seconds.

141

One hundred yards into my first mile of marathon training I had to stop. The combination of the sun and my pace had knocked me to my knees. Not a figurative knocked to my knees, but a literal knocked to my knees. I had ran 100 yards and had to kneel down and catch my breath.

I turned around and went back to the house defeated. How was I going to run 26.2 miles if I couldn't go 100 yards? I knew something had to change, and I knew I needed a plan.

I called people I knew who had finished a marathon and got some advice. I went to a running store and got correct shoes and clothes. I read a few running books and learned how to pace myself.

One of the running books I came across encouraged me to ACT on my goals during training. ACT is a fancy acronym that helps break down an Impossible Dream by making sure it is:

- **Achievable**
- **Concrete**
- **Timed**

Not only did I have to learn how to run long distances, I had to memorize acronyms as well? I reached for my donut to calm my nerves...this was going to be a long journey.

A - Achievable

The first thing I found while learning about how to ACT on my goals was that I couldn't actually run 26.2 miles. I couldn't even walk 26.2 miles. My impossible dream would eventually be achievable, but it wasn't actually achievable at that moment. I had to make my initial goals something I could do without passing out on the hot Tulsa concrete.

I still had my Impossible Dream of completing a marathon, but I made my first achievable goal to finish the Race for the Cure 5k in one month. The goal was actually achievable. It wouldn't be easy, but I could do it.

I followed my plan to perfection, and I finished my first 5k about 2 months into training. I followed the tortoise strategy of being slow and steady. I assumed that anything that worked for the tortoise would work for me.

My next goal was a 10k. Boom, accomplished.
Then I decided I wanted to finish a 15k. Guess what?? Domination.

Next goal? Half marathon.
I trained for and ran a half-marathon with Kristin at the Route 66 in Tulsa, and finished without keeling over.

I found that running a half marathon was not only achievable, it was fun! I met great friends and actually loved learning about running strategies and running with different types of people.

C- Concrete

My Impossible Dream was too broad and needed to be narrowed down. I did that by making it Achievable and building towards my ID of running a marathon.

After the joy of finishing a half-marathon wore off, I learned that training for a full marathon was much more challenging than training for a half. Saturday morning runs went from lasting two hours to lasting five hours. I spent more time being sore than I spent not being sore. I even started doing the marathon walk, which is a fancy thing marathoners do after a particularly hard run where they walk a little bowl-legged, and mostly in a crooked line.

I needed my training to be more concrete. I really needed a solid and unwavering plan that helped me lay the foundation to achieve my ID.

I was going to run four days a week, following the schedule that had been customized for me from a running group in Tulsa. I would be specific about the time of the day I ran and keep track of my process. I would even track the food I ate during my marathon training. Later I found that marathoners called food fuel, and it made me feel cooler when I tracked my fuel. I was becoming a cold-blooded running machine.

Over the next few months I learned about ice baths, busted toenails, and the problem with introducing new fuel into your diet pre-run. Every Sunday I felt exhausted from the fatigue of running 50-60 miles a week.

As I progressed in my journey to run a marathon and check off my ID, I altered the plan and adjusted if necessary. It was not easy and sometimes not fun, but it was worth it. I had a great plan that would help me do the unachievable. I could look at my wife and proudly tell her that I was working hard on something that mattered.

Eventually, my training started to pay off. I got faster, stronger, and leaner. I felt so good about the way I felt and the way that I looked that I didn't even feel the need to stop by QuikTrip for a tasty donut.

T - Timed

Finally, It was time for me to buck up and pick a race. The last step in ACTing on my goal was to make it time-bound. I needed an end date to my training to make my goal a reality. I picked the Oklahoma City Memorial Marathon in April of 2009, a little more than 10 years after the car accident that changed my life forever.

When race day came, I was nervous but confident. There were tens of thousands of people lined up at the start line, and I couldn't help but feel a sense of pride gathered around so many motivated athletes. Regardless of the outcome of the race, I had accomplished the hardest part of a marathon, the training.

I had learned how to ACT on my Impossible Dream and plan out my journey. I had stuck to a plan and developed the willpower to follow through with my ambition. **I was going to *Live My List* by achieving the hardest bucket on my list.**

I experienced every emotion possible during the marathon...joy, anger, sadness, frustration, fatigue, pain, and finally elation. Ten years after my wreck I had run a full marathon, something the doctors would have never guessed.

I moved on to run 3 more marathons, and even ran one in Beijing, China, where we started at Tiananmen Square and finished in the Olympic Village, on the track that the Olympic marathoners had run 2 years prior. I have since ran a 4:48 mile, an 18:28 5k, a 1:38 half marathon and a 3:41 full marathon.

Running has taught me discipline, determination, dedication, and perseverance. It brought a sense of mental toughness and follow-through I had never had in my life. I was able to keep going when I thought I could not possibly go any further. It has given me a sense of pride and confidence in myself that will never be shaken.

I want you to feel the same sense of achievement and purpose that I felt throughout my marathoning journey.

TAKE YOUR ID AND ACT ON IT BY FILLING OUT THE FOLLOWING ITEMS.

A - Achievable

Break your ID into smaller goals that you can achieve. Make the goals sequential so they will get harder and harder to achieve as you build to your Impossible Dream.

_____

_____

_____

_____

_____

_____

_____

C - Concrete

What is your concrete plan to make your Impossible Dream a reality?
Be as specific as possible.

_____

_____

_____

_____

_____

_____

_____

_____

T - Timed

When will you achieve your ID? Put an end-date and make it a reality!

_____

_____

_____

_____

_____

_____

_____

_____

_____

live
YOUR
list

CHART YOUR TIME

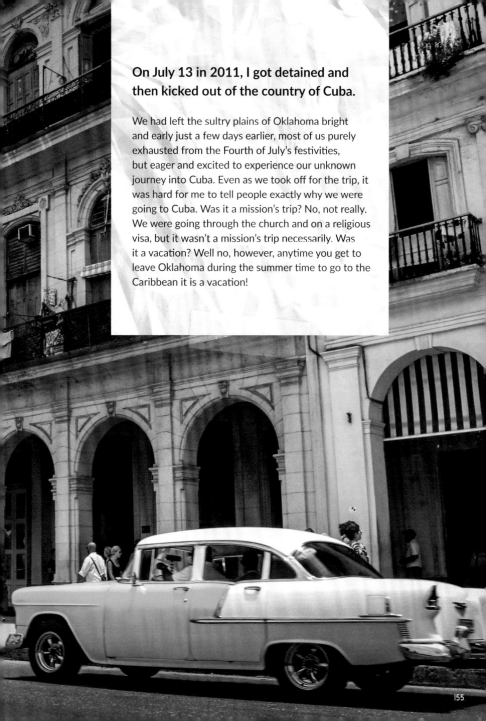

On July 13 in 2011, I got detained and then kicked out of the country of Cuba.

We had left the sultry plains of Oklahoma bright and early just a few days earlier, most of us purely exhausted from the Fourth of July's festivities, but eager and excited to experience our unknown journey into Cuba. Even as we took off for the trip, it was hard for me to tell people exactly why we were going to Cuba. Was it a mission's trip? No, not really. We were going through the church and on a religious visa, but it wasn't a mission's trip necessarily. Was it a vacation? Well no, however, anytime you get to leave Oklahoma during the summer time to go to the Caribbean it is a vacation!

The best answer I could provide then, even as we waited to board the plane to Miami, was that we were going to host a leadership conference for Cuban youth ministers. Our team's reason for going wasn't too far off from that original thought, but it was so much more than that simple answer.

The "Dream Team," as Murr called us, included myself,* Jerrod, founder of Believing in a Better Way and the brains behind this trip, Darrin, Senior Pastor at Morris First Assembly of God (also, my former roommate, husband of Sarah, and Phantom of the Opera lover), Mario, former Youth Pastor at Muldrow Assembly of God and token interpreter for our trip, Aaron, AKA A-Mo, computer nerd extraordinaire and resident heart-throb, and Josh, husband of Jill and brother of Jerrod, who owns about seven thousand rental homes.

* If you don't know me by now...

We landed in Miami and boarded a charter flight to Cuba. We were the only people on the plane who weren't Cubans. After a safe takeoff the crowd erupted in a roar of applause, which we found repeated after we quickly landed in Cuba. On a personal side note, it was a fun tradition I think I will continue on all my travels, until some American travelers throw their lattes on me because they have to update their Facebook and Twitter without distraction.

After landing in Cuba to a rousing round of applause from our plane companions, we quickly got off of the plane so we could get through customs and safely meet with our drivers. Once we made it to customs I found it is much like American travel, a whole lot of "hurry up and wait." We stood in line with the other travelers and their TVs, waiting to go through the single security checkpoint at the Cuban airport.

This is when we got into a sticky situation.

The conference organizers had asked if we could bring giveaways for the conference attendees. Cubans love music so we thought we should bring some instruments, CDs, and MP3 players. Most of those items were cheap and small enough to pack in our suitcases. Not one member of the Dream Team stopped to think about the trade embargo the United States had with Cuba.

Unfortunately for us, the Cuban version of the TSA had not forgotten about the embargo. They pulled Jerrod aside and asked him to explain the technology. When I say they pulled him aside, I mean they took him into an interrogation room and sought answers.

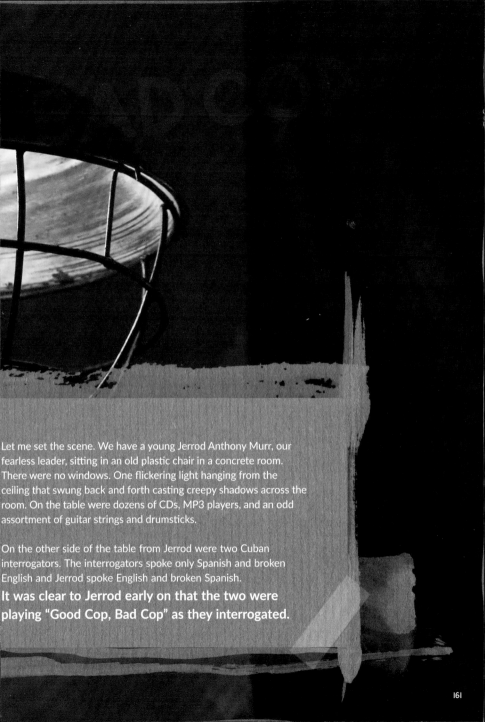

Let me set the scene. We have a young Jerrod Anthony Murr, our fearless leader, sitting in an old plastic chair in a concrete room. There were no windows. One flickering light hanging from the ceiling that swung back and forth casting creepy shadows across the room. On the table were dozens of CDs, MP3 players, and an odd assortment of guitar strings and drumsticks.

On the other side of the table from Jerrod were two Cuban interrogators. The interrogators spoke only Spanish and broken English and Jerrod spoke English and broken Spanish. **It was clear to Jerrod early on that the two were playing "Good Cop, Bad Cop" as they interrogated.**

Due to the language barrier, Jerrod couldn't quite understand what they were saying to him, but he knew one was aggressive and one was kind-hearted. One would slam his fist on the table and raise his voice. Immediately afterwards the other one would talk with a soft voice and place his hand on Jerrod's shoulder.

This routine continued for almost a half hour, and the entire time Jerrod kept repeating, "No habla espanol" and "son regalos." These were the two phrases Jerrod had learned from his previous trip to Cuba. *Son regalos* roughly translates into "these are gifts."

Whatever Jerrod did or said, it worked. He got one last tongue lashing from the bad cop as the interrogator stormed out of the room. The good cop walked over to Jerrod, placed a hand on his shoulder, and spoke quietly for a couple minutes before he left Jerrod alone in the room.

Another Cuban walked into the room, put all of our giveaways into the suitcase, and handed it to Jerrod. She then led Jerrod back to the rest of us waiting outside of the airport. Jerrod told us to get in the car and leave immediately before they changed their minds. We were literally followed the rest of our trip. Everywhere we went we had people gathering surveillance on our team.

Regardless, we made our way to the hotel and then to the conference. The backdrop of our conference was breathtaking. The beautiful landscapes beyond the fence, the generous shrubbery, the banana and mango trees offering us shade from the glaring Caribbean sun. These mango trees littered the ground with ripe and delicious fruit that made for wonderful juggling balls. I had somewhat learned to juggle on a Bucket List trip that my beautiful wife planned for me, but I was certainly a novice.

Josh, A-Mo, and I were tossing some mangos around when we learned we had a juggling master in our midst. This Cuban, named Ernesto, was a skilled juggler and had taught many, many people how to juggle. He walked up to me and said I was juggling all wrong. He took two mangos out of my hands and placed them on the ground.

He set us all up with mangos and explained to us that juggling is not about mastering three balls at one time, but mastering one. We started with one mango, and didn't move on to juggling the next until we could easily, almost inherently juggle with one mango. He said juggling mangos is like juggling time. You can not move onto another task until you have mastered the first. If you try to take on too many tasks at once you will drop all your responsibilities and fail.

This is a lesson I have carried with me ever since. Never take on more than you can juggle. Master one thing before trying to master three. Be careful to manage the tasks you have in front of you so you don't waste your time.

Every once in awhile, I would drop my mango and the other Dream Team members would laugh at me. Ernesto would quickly scold them in Spanish and then tell us to never laugh at those trying to learn. He said in broken English,

LAUGH AT YOUR MISTAKES, AND MOST IMPORTANTLY, LEARN FROM OTHERS.

You will find a day when you are learning something new and you will want others to show you grace.

Once we mastered juggling one mango, we moved to two mangos. We spent hours under the Caribbean sun throwing two mangos back and forth between our hands until we were masters. Then he handed us our third mango.

He assured us that we had the tools necessary to succeed as a juggler. We had worked hard to master the technique. All we had to do now is let muscle memory kick in and start juggling! He was completely right, it took me only a few times to become a juggler. From that day on I have been able to juggle. The foundations of juggling we learned in Cuba have stuck with me throughout the years.

My experience in Cuba made me question how I viewed my time. At this point I had been living my list for almost eight years. I had traveled to several continents and starting working as a full time professional. I had started a side business and it was going well. I was married to the hottest woman on the planet and we were expecting our first child.

Life was great, but my time management was not.

If I wanted to live my list and make a difference, I needed to do a better job managing my time. So I started by charting my time. I took out a pen and paper and made a graph that had 24 one-hour time slots. For the next month I tracked every hour of my day. Somedays I tracked it more closely than others, but I accounted for all of my time.

I challenge you to do the same. Take the following chart and track your time for at least one week. If you prefer to do it digitally, that is OK too. I have found several apps that do a great job tracking time.

- ATracker - *wonderapps.se/atracker/*
- Hours - *hourstimetracking.com*
- Everhour - *everhour.com*

Chart Your Day

24 hours for one week

12:00 a.m.		12:00 p.m.	
12:30 a.m.		12:30 p.m.	
1:00 a.m.		1:00 p.m.	
1:30 a.m.		1:30 p.m.	
2:00 a.m.		2:00 p.m.	
2:30 a.m.		2:30 p.m.	
3:00 a.m		3:00 p.m	
3:30 a.m.		3:30 p.m.	
4:00 a.m.		4:00 p.m.	
4:30 a.m.		4:30 p.m.	
5:00 a.m.		5:00 p.m.	
5:30 a.m.		5:30 p.m.	
6:00 a.m.		6:00 p.m.	
6:30 a.m.		6:30 p.m.	
7:00 a.m.		7:00 p.m.	
7:30 a.m.		7:30 p.m.	
8:00 a.m.		8:00 p.m.	
8:30 a.m.		8:30 p.m.	
9:00 a.m.		9:00 p.m.	
9:30 a.m.		9:30 p.m.	
10:00 a.m.		10:00 p.m.	
10:30 a.m.		10:30 p.m.	
11:00 a.m.		11:00 p.m.	
11:30 a.m.		11:30 p.m.	

live
YOUR
list

FOUR
QUADRANTS

Essentials	Hustle
Interruptions	**Time Sucks**

After I tracked my time for one month, I started to notice a trend: every moment of time I tracked fell into one of four categories.

Quadrant 1 - Essentials

These were things that I had to do. If I did not complete these tasks there were immediate consequences. These included sleeping, eating, working, going to class, paying bills, etc. If I did not go to work I could get fired. If I did not sleep my body would break down. If I did not eat I would starve.

Quadrant 2 - Hustle

These were things that helped me get better. If I did not complete these tasks there were not immediate consequences, but there were long-term implications. This included exercising, planning, studying, resting, family time, vacations, organizing, etc. If I did not exercise, I wouldn't immediately suffer, but over a long time it would make my life much more challenging.

Quadrant 3 - Interruptions

These were the annoying things that kept me from getting stuff done. Sometimes it was a flat tire or repairing a broken phone. Other times it was unexpected visitors or busy work for my class. Regardless of these tasks, at the end of the time spent on interruptions, I was no closer to achieving my impossible dream than before I started.

Quadrant 4 - Time Sucks

I spent a considerable amount of time doing nothing or wasting time. These were items that not only didn't get me closer to living my list, but also didn't help me become a better person. Instead of watching one OKC Thunder game, I watched three a week. Instead of checking Facebook for a few minutes I checked Facebook for an hour. Don't get me started about the time I wasted on Snapchat, Twitter, or Reddit.

After you have analyzed your time for an entire week, I want you to come back to this page and place your time into the four categories. Go ahead, put the book down and track your time. Actually, don't put down the book in case you don't pick it back up. Instead, go grab a sticky note and place it on the side of this page. Make a note in your calendar for you to come back and complete this task in one week. After all, we are trying to master our time. This will be good practice!

Quadrant 1 | ESSENTIALS

Manage these tasks. When you are doing these things, try to do them as efficiently as possible. If you commute to work everyday, find the fastest route. If you have to do homework or an assignment, put aside all distractions and get it done as fast (and as well) as possible.

1.   Urgent phone calls or emails

2.   Meetings

3.   Family emergencies

Quadrant 2 | HUSTLE

Maximize these tasks. These are the things that will make you better in the long run. If you spend a free hour organizing then the next time you have to put things up it will be more efficient which will allow you to spend more time hustlin'. Make sure your recreation items do not cross over into time sucks. If recreation becomes an obsession you are wasting time.

1.   Exercise
2.   Goal setting
3.   Reading

Quadrant 3 | INTERRUPTIONS

Minimize your distractions. If you consistently find yourself getting interrupted then create better boundaries. Find a better place to work or study. Talk to people who are wasting your time and try to find ways to minimize bad relationships. You will never eliminate all interruptions but you can minimize them as you *Live Your List*.

1.   Off-task phone calls & emails

2.   Constantly checking your phone

3.   Excessive time on a task that is fairly unimportant

Quadrant 4 | TIME SUCKS

Eliminate your time wasters. These are things that do not help you *Live Your List* or achieve your Impossible Dream. Just let them go.

1. Video games
2. Mindless social media browsing
3. Reddit

When I was juggling in Cuba I learned to master multiple things at one time. As you continue to *Live Your List* you will find that the more you try to change the world the more time you must juggle. It is a constant improvement process that never becomes perfect.

As of the writing of this book I have the hottest wife in the world, two wonderful children, run a business with 50 employees, and have multiple side projects. On top off all of the essential tasks I have to manage, I still need to find time to hustle and avoid interruptions and time sucks.

I hope that in 20 years I am still trying to change the world and live my list while consistently achieving Impossible Dreams. This means I will constantly work on managing my time. With each new task, I will learn to master what I am already doing and then add one more juggling ball to the mix.

Once I master my time I can focus on things that matter much more... like Finding my Verb.

live
YOUR
list

FIND
YOUR
VERB

It wasn't until I got back into the office that I found out my pants were unzipped. I was 23 years old and freshly out of college. I was in love with my dream gal and had just started my first big kid job. There was a ton of responsibility with my new big kid job, and leaving my fly open was not on the job description.

I have had a job for as long as I can remember, but I had never had a big kid job. My first jobs were part-time or working for family. My actual first job (outside of milking cows for my family) was being an "elf" at the Arrowhead Mall in Muskogee, OK during Christmastime. My responsibilities included, but we were not limited to taking pictures of kids while they cried on Santa's lap, operating the Christmas train, and occasionally cleaning up after the leaky kiddos that frequent Santa's workshop.

I even once had to fill in as Santa when the "professional" Santa didn't show up for work. There were three elves available to be Santa on that particular night: me or my sisters Leslie and Melissa. They voted against me (typical) and I was slated to become that night's Santa Claus.

STEP ONE:
CHECK
YOUR FLY.

179

I was a fresh-faced 15 year old that was not far removed from my horrendous car accident. I had gained some weight back by Christmas, but I only weighed about 150 pounds. I don't know if you know this, but most Santas are depicted as chubby and jolly. I was not chubby and not particularly jolly when I looked at myself in the mirror while wearing a Santa suit.

I looked like a Santa going through chemotherapy. The red coat hung off of my narrow shoulders like a deflated tent. The belt was too big for me to even buckle. The only thing saving me was the suspenders that kept my pants from dropping to the ground.

Regardless, I was committed to my job and walked into Santa's Workshop with a forced smile and a hearty "Ho, Ho, Ho!" The parents waiting in line looked a little mortified as "Cancer Santa" sat down in the big chair and welcomed the first scared child.

The little kid sat on my lap and immediately started to get shifty on me. I asked him what he wanted for Christmas, and he grimaced as he said he wanted a Furby.* I didn't understand why the kid was acting like he was in so much pain, and I wanted to ask if he was OK.

I had always heard stories about Santas and other everyday superheroes who saved kids from domestic abuse or bullying through their make-believe character. This was my chance to really make a difference in this kid's life. It was going to be a Christmas Miracle.

I leaned in gently and in my most Santa-like impression said, "Little Jimmy** you know you can tell Santa anything. If you are sick, hurting, or even if anyone is causing you pain you know you can tell me!"

---

* It was 1998. Don't judge the kid too harshly.

** Name has been changed to protect the innocent.

He looked relieved and leaned towards me and said,

"SANTA, YOUR KNEE IS REALLY BONY AND IT IS HURTING ME. YOU SHOULD PROBABLY GAIN SOME WEIGHT."

It's official. I was the worst Santa of all-time. I was even worse than the drunk Santa in "The Miracle on 34th Street." I immediately retired and moved on to my next job. I was the Easter Bunny that Spring.

A few more of my early jobs and a few key takeaways:

- **Janitor at a Trucking Industry** - After cleaning toilets I realized most truckers have incredibly unhealthy diets. If you are a trucker you probably need help.

- **Dollar Rent-A-Car Call Center** - Customers do not think it's funny if you answer the phone in weird accents.

- **Milker on a Dairy Farm** - Women don't like it when you compare them to cattle.

- **Night Shift Attendant at Holiday Inn** - My only real responsibility was setting up the breakfast bar for the morning. I love breakfast and ate it as fast as I set it out.

- **Assembly Line at a Paper Factory** - They do not think it is funny when you break their safety record by goofing around.

- **Bus Repair** - This job only lasted one week. I was not good at this job.

- **Campus Tour Guide** - I took this job to meet the ladies.

You would think with all of the extensive and varied job experience that I had over the years that I would remember to do something as simple as zipping up my pants before I gave a presentation to over 500 ninth graders.

I worked for Educational Talent Search at my alma mater, Northeastern State University, in Tahlequah, OK. I was a guidance counselor with the goal of helping first-generation, low-income high school students get into some sort of post-secondary education. If they wanted to go to Harvard, we got them into Harvard. If they wanted to get into the local welding school, we got them into the local welding school.

It was an awesome job.

One of our responsibilities was to go to high schools and recruit participants for the program. This included us giving impassioned speeches to large groups of ninth graders, and then to walk them through the application process. We would then go back to the office and review the applications and select the future participants.

It was when I was back in the office I realized my fly was down. I had given an hour long speech, helped students individually, talked to the administrators,

AND EVEN HAD LUNCH WITH MY ZIPPER ALL THE WAY DOWN.

It really didn't matter though, because I loved my job. They let me talk in front of large groups. I got to create interactive and engaging curriculum. I had wonderful coworkers and loved my students. They even gave me a check with a comma in it...so of course I had to throw a comma party.

For the uninitiated, a comma party is for individuals who finally have a check large enough to include a comma. Up until my 23rd year on earth, I had never received a check more than $999. **My comma party was glorious and short-lived as I realized I also had bills to pay.**

One of the best parts of my job was that it helped me find my purpose.

Now, let me be clear. It helped me find my purpose. Not necessarily my passion. Not necessarily my career (even though it helped me with those too). It helped me find my purpose.

Growing up, I always heard that I needed to pursue my purpose. Or was it to follow my passion? Or find my dream career? Or maybe it was to passionately and purposely find my career.

AS YOU
COULD TELL
I WAS
CONFUSED.

Even as a young professional I had read countless books during my hustle time that mixed up passion, career, and purpose. So, I set out to understand for myself the differences in the words. I turned to the wisest Jerrod that I knew - Jerrod Anthony Murr.*

Now, you know Murr and you love him. Well, you may not know him, but if you did you would love him. I know I certainly do.

I have known of Jerrod my entire life. My dad rode the school bus with Jerrod's mom back in the 1960s. My grandpa bought his dairy farm from Jerrod's grandpa. Jerrod's dad worked on my grandpa's dairy farm with my dad. Needless to say, the Ellers and the Murrs go way back.

---

* He is also the only Jerrod I know, but that's beside the point.

FIND
YOUR
VERB

I didn't really get to know Jerrod until the Fall of 2000 when we went on the world's worst double date. I am the reason the date was terrible. I may or may not have called my girlfriend by the wrong name.*

The date ended with Jerrod and me going to a movie together and sharing popcorn. On second thought, Jerrod and I had a wonderful date... it was the ladies that had a bad date.

The rest of our timeline looks like this:

*   Spoiler alert: I definitely called her the wrong name.

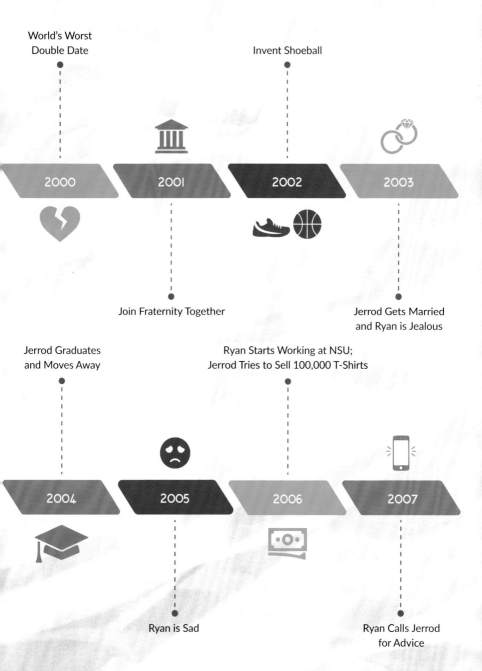

World's Worst Double Date

Invent Shoeball

2000

2001

2002

2003

Join Fraternity Together

Jerrod Gets Married and Ryan is Jealous

Jerrod Graduates and Moves Away

Ryan Starts Working at NSU; Jerrod Tries to Sell 100,000 T-Shirts

2004

2005

2006

2007

Ryan is Sad

Ryan Calls Jerrod for Advice

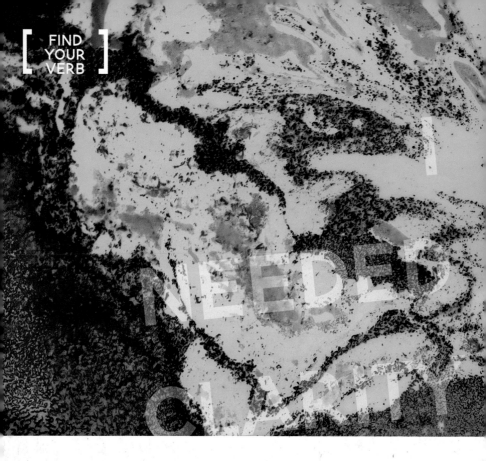

I called Jerrod for advice in 2007 because I needed some clarity. I felt secure in my job at Northeastern State University. I loved my students, my co-workers, and working for my alma mater. I was very comfortable.

But there was something missing. I felt called to do more. I had started facilitating leadership workshops for high school groups and I loved it. I felt like that was my purpose in life. Or my passion. Potentially my dream career. I really didn't know.

IT'S WHY I CALLED MURR.

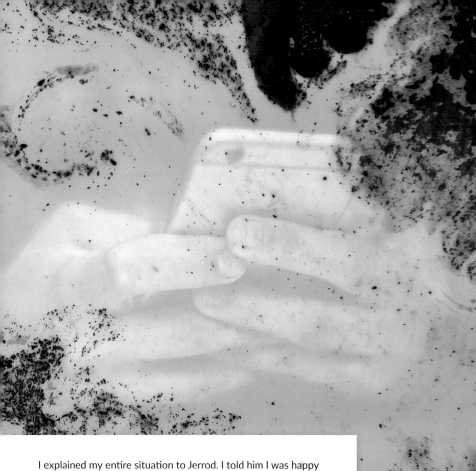

I explained my entire situation to Jerrod. I told him I was happy but felt called to do more to make a difference in people's lives. That I loved my job but also felt like I needed to pursue this side job facilitating leadership workshops. I needed his advice.

I've said Jerrod was like Forrest Gump's mom, he always had a way of explaining things so I could understand them.

FIND
YOUR
VERB

JERROD ARGUED THAT
OUR PURPOSE IS NOT
A NOUN – A PERSON,
PLACE, OR THING.

Nouns as our purpose are too narrow of a scope, and the nouns in our life change. Just in my short life I have changed jobs multiple times*, have been in and out of relationships, and moved locations. If my purpose was wrapped up in any of those things, I would be completely lost when the noun changed.

He said we need to view our purpose as a verb.

Our purpose is a large and overarching theme throughout our life. A verb is used to describe an action, state, or occurrence. So, if our purpose is a verb it means that we are taking action! We are doing something. Instead of our purpose being a person, place, or thing, it could be to act, play, encourage, motivate, inspire, or fix. It could be to love, create, align, save, reconcile, or mentor.

Still, I wasn't exactly understanding, so ~~Mama Gump~~ Jerrod told me to close my eyes and imagine a car going down a big road. I encourage you to do the same.

Well, keep your eyes open unless you can get someone to read this book to you.

---

* Remember when I was the Easter Bunny?

Imagine a car going down a road.
The road you are traveling on is long and winding and
never-ending. The road is your purpose. It is broad and
you will always be pursuing the destination at the end of
the road - a purpose-filled life.

It is utterly important to determine that you are on the
right road. I think there have been many people (myself
included) who choose to travel down the wrong road by
trying to find their purpose in a person, place, or thing.

I CHALLENGE YOU TO
THINK OF YOUR PURPOSE
AS A VERB INSTEAD.

The beauty of traveling through life pursuing a verb is that you can find your purpose in almost any scenario. If my verb is to empower, I can empower in almost all roles of my life. I can empower as a husband, a father, a leadership facilitator, a friend, or even in line at Walmart.

Jerrod then continued with the metaphor. He
explained that the vehicles on the road represent the
roles that define our life (the nouns). We will travel
through life using many vehicles. As mentioned above,
the vehicle you chose to pursue your purpose may
be as a spouse, son, daughter, grandparent, caregiver,
friend, employee, boss, stranger, volunteer, counselor,
author, coach, or consultant.

**Honestly, we all have many different roles
in life and they will change over time.**

Jerrod encouraged me to choose my vehicles wisely.
The roles in which I spend the majority of my life need
to help me pursue my purpose and live out my verb. I
can honestly say that the most fulfillment I have found
as a spouse is when I have empowered Kristin to live
life to the fullest. As a father, I feel most fulfilled when
I empower Jane and Caleb to learn new things or meet
new people. As a facilitator, I feel fulfilled when I can
empower a group to be the best version of themselves
and see leadership a little bit differently.

CHOOSE
WISELY

GASOLINE

FUEL YOUR PASSION

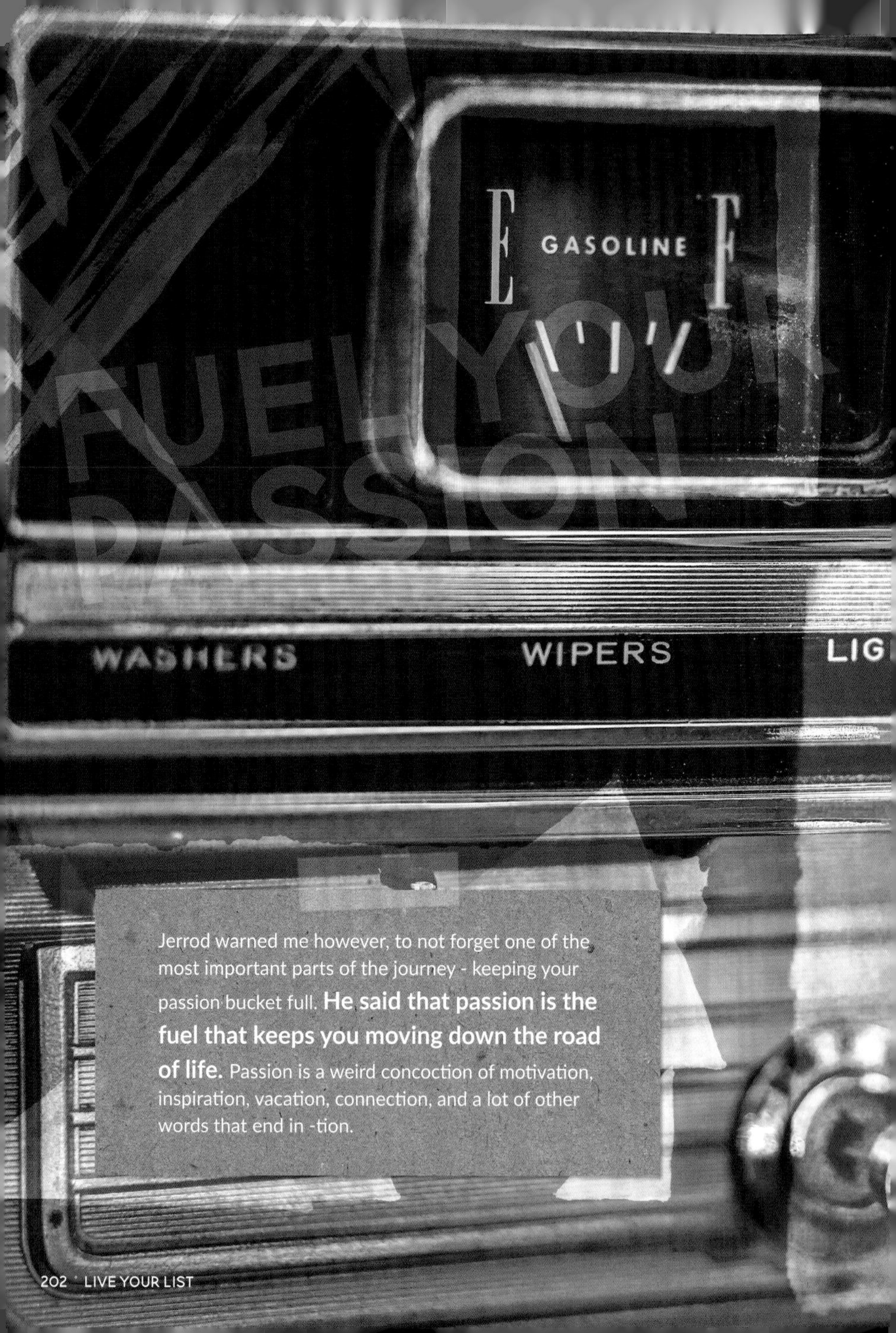

WASHERS   WIPERS   LIG

Jerrod warned me however, to not forget one of the most important parts of the journey - keeping your passion bucket full. **He said that passion is the fuel that keeps you moving down the road of life.** Passion is a weird concoction of motivation, inspiration, vacation, connection, and a lot of other words that end in -tion.

Your vehicle needs fuel to travel down the road, and the larger the vehicle the more fuel it requires. You might have experienced this before. Imagine this scenario - you get a promotion and a raise at work. With the promotion comes extra responsibility. You are excited about the responsibility though, because you know this new job will help you fulfill your purpose.

YOUR PASSION BUCKET IS FULL.

The first few months you work extra hard to make the transition go smoothly. You have to spend some nights and weekends taking care of the paperwork that was left undone by the previous employee. Other co-workers have been overworked and they ask you to help. You feel obligated to take more of the workload since you have been given the promotion.

After a few months of this you start to get fatigued. You are easily annoyed. Your home life is struggling.
You do not enjoy your work responsibilities anymore.

You have run out of fuel;

YOU HAVE RUN OUT OF PASSION.

Jerrod reminded me that if I wanted to pursue this new career with my side job, Paradigm Shift, that I would need to constantly add more fuel to my passion bucket. I would need to find ways to rest and recoup. I would need to be intentional to celebrate my small victories and continuously learn new things.

The larger the vehicle the more fuel you will need. Some of us are driving school buses (literally and figuratively) with loads of people and we need to constantly refuel. Some people are driving high-octane race cars and need special fuel. Others are driving a Prius and are efficiently cruising down the road of life.

ALWAYS MAKE SURE YOUR PASSION BUCKET IS FULL.

He even continued the metaphor to encourage me to find the right people to ride in the car with me while I fulfilled my purpose. You know how some people are good road trip partners? Some people pick the right playlist, make things easier for you as you drive, and hand feed you road trip food?

Other passengers are absolutely the worst. They stop to go to the restroom every few hours. They never offer to drive and always sleep. They don't hand feed you your road trip snacks.*

* People don't hand feed you?

GUARD YOUR PASSION

Just like in real life, people can siphon your fuel.
They can steal your passion.
Guard your passion from those with intent to harm you.

Feel free to give your passion away, but

MAKE SURE YOU STILL HAVE ENOUGH TO TRAVEL YOUR JOURNEY.

I told you Jerrod was great at explaining things. So much so that I decided to go into business with him. I spent the next five years side-by-side with Jerrod building a business: Paradigm Shift. We traveled from state to state and eventually from country to country to teach leadership lessons to all age groups.

We both worked two full-time jobs during those five years. We also had children, experienced loss, and overcame adversity. We made mistakes and learned from them. These were some of the most amazing years of our young lives.

During that time I found true fulfillment from finding my verb. I learned how to empower during my time as a guidance counselor in TRIO at NSU. I also found out how to maximize it through my part-time job with Paradigm Shift.

The lessons we learned about purpose and passion during this time has never left us. There are times when our passion bucket is low and we take a break. There are other times when we have gotten away from our primary purpose and need to refocus on what really matters.

In 2013 I left my job at NSU to pursue my purpose of empowering people. The best career vehicle for me to pursue that purpose was as a leadership facilitator, keynote speaker, and corporate trainer.

The catalyst for me to live my list inside of my career was to find my verb.

I would like to empower you to do the same.* On the next few pages we have lists of verbs. Spend some time reflecting on the times you have felt most fulfilled. What were you doing during those times? What verb matches your actions? Find and circle those verbs. You may find 100 verbs. You may only find one. Both are OK. Feel free to write in your own verbs if they are missing from the page.

_____

_____

_____

_____

_____

_____

_____

_____

* See what I did there? I am so fulfilled right now.

ACCELERATE	ENCOURAGE	LEAD	SEE
ACT	ENGINEER	LIFT	SHAPE
ADAPT	ENTERTAIN	LINK	SHOW
ADMIRE	EMPOWER	LIST	SIMULATE
ADVANCE	EXCITE	LIVE	SING
ALTER	EXECUTE	LOVE	SPIRIT
AMPLIFY	EXPAND	MAKE	SPRINT
ASK	EXPEDITE	MAP	START
ASTONISH	EXPLAIN	MASTER	STEAL
AUTHORIZE	EXPLORE	MOTIVATE	STIMULATE
BARGAIN	FIX	MULTIPLY	STREAMLINE
BOOST	FLY	NAVIGATE	SUGGEST
BUILD	FOCUS	NURTURE	SUPPORT
CHALLENGE	FREE	OFFER	SURPRISE
CHEER	GAIN	OPERATE	TEACH
CLEAN	GAMBLE	ORGANIZE	TEST
COACH	GENERATE	OVERHAUL	THINK
COLLECT	GIVE	PLAN	TRACK
COMPETE	GO	PRESENT	TRAIN
CONNECT	GRAB	PRODUCE	TREASURE
CONVERT	GRASP	PROFIT	TRIUMPH
CRAFT	GUARANTEE	PROMOTE	TRY
CREATE	GUIDE	PROPOSE	UNITE
DEFY	HELP	PROTECT	UPDATE
DELIVER	HINT	PROVE	UPGRADE
DEMONSTRATE	HOLD	REDUCE	USE
DESCRIBE	IMPACT	RESPOND	VALIDATE
DESIGN	INSIST	REVAMP	VERIFY
DETECT	INSPIRE	REVEAL	WIN
DIRECT	INVENT	RUN	WONDER
DRIVE	JOIN	SAVE	WORK
EDUCATE	LAUNCH	SECURE	WRITE

Verb Tournament

Find your top eight verbs and randomly insert them into the bracket below. Spend time contemplating which verbs finds you the most fulfillment.

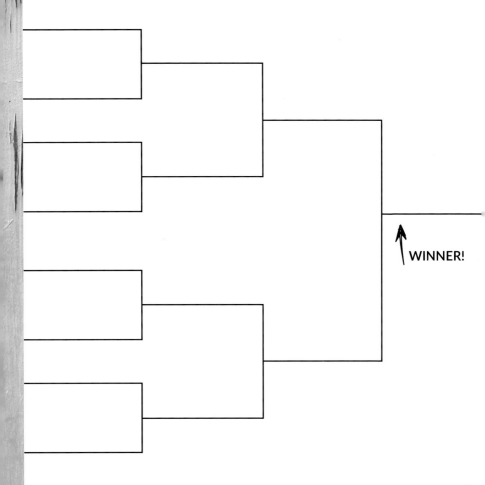

WINNER!

Determine Your Vehicles

What different roles do you have in life? Write down every single role you can use to pursue your purpose and *Live Your List.*

Role 1: _____

Role 2: _____

Role 3: _____

Role 4: _____

Role 5: _____

Role 6: _____

Role 7: _____

Role 8: _____

Role 9: _____

Role 10: _____

Role 11: _____

Role 12: _____

Role 13: _____

Role 14: _____

Role 15: _____

Role 16: _____

Role 17: _____

Role 18: _____

Role 19: _____

Role 20: _____

Role 21: _____

Role 22: _____

Role 23: _____

Role 24: _____

Role 25: _____

Ways to Keep your Passion Bucket Full

List all of the different ways you can keep your passion bucket full!

_____

_____

_____

_____

_____

_____

_____

_____

_____

_____

_____

_____

_____

_____

_____

_____

_____

_____

_____

_____

My verb is to empower. Jerrod's verb is to create.

We are the most energized when we are acting through our verbs. Your verb may look very different. Regardless, it is important that you never stop trying to pursue your purpose as you *Live Your List*.

Once you find your verb you can then move to the next level. It is during the next phase that incredible growth will occur. It certainly was true for me. We watched Paradigm Shift grow from two guys working out of spare bedrooms to a million dollar organization. We parlay all of our opportunities into the next big leaps of living our list.

live YOUR list

PARLAY

As a traveling Paradigm Shift facilitator, I met some awesome people. Here are a few highlights of the unique people in some of my workshops:*

- **Roy the Golden Child** - Roy was a 10-foot, two-ton monster who showered in vodka and fed his babies shrimp scampi. He could palm a medicine ball and owned a pet snake. He was a unique dude.

- **Zach from St. Louis** - Zach was once accused of trying to blow up the St. Louis arch and had visited more than 50 countries from across the world.

- **Stephinfection** - Stephinfection had awesome hair and knew every single word to every single Disney movie ever.

- **Cousin Amy** - She had more cousins than anyone else in history. Everyone called her Cousin Amy, including us.

- **Philip the Bright** - There wasn't really anything crazy about Philip, but I liked him none-the-less.

Neha,
Technically an American

---

* All identities below have been changed to protect the innocent.

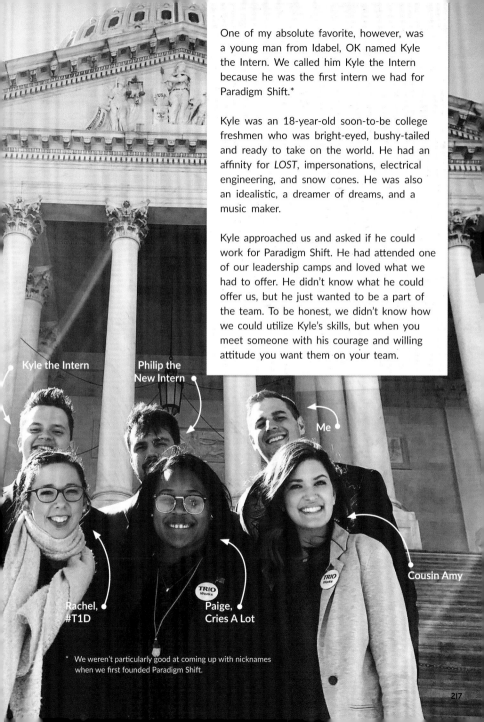

One of my absolute favorite, however, was a young man from Idabel, OK named Kyle the Intern. We called him Kyle the Intern because he was the first intern we had for Paradigm Shift.*

Kyle was an 18-year-old soon-to-be college freshmen who was bright-eyed, bushy-tailed and ready to take on the world. He had an affinity for *LOST*, impersonations, electrical engineering, and snow cones. He was also an idealistic, a dreamer of dreams, and a music maker.

Kyle approached us and asked if he could work for Paradigm Shift. He had attended one of our leadership camps and loved what we had to offer. He didn't know what he could offer us, but he just wanted to be a part of the team. To be honest, we didn't know how we could utilize Kyle's skills, but when you meet someone with his courage and willing attitude you want them on your team.

Kyle the Intern

Philip the New Intern

Me

Cousin Amy

Rachel, #T1D

Paige, Cries A Lot

* We weren't particularly good at coming up with nicknames when we first founded Paradigm Shift.

We figured the best use of Kyle's talent would be to hire him as a driver. I am sure you noticed in his skill sets above that we didn't mention professional driver. However, there was an incredible amount of need for one.

I had been traveling all year from state to state leading events. I would spend five hours leading a workshop on Monday and then drive eight hours to my next workshop on Tuesday. Then I would spend Wednesday and Thursday in a new location and drive eight hours home on Friday. I did this for nearly a year before my body started to shut down on me.

I was mentally, emotionally, physically, and spiritually ➤ **EXHAUSTED.**

It became increasingly harder and harder for me to make it to the next location.

The most direct need was for Kyle to drive me around and keep me company. It was however, not his only responsibility. He also was in charge of the following tasks:

- **Pillow fluffer** - Kyle would fluff my pillow every night to make sure it was the perfect level of fluffiness.
- **Food tester** - Just in case one of my clients were poisoning me, Kyle would test all of my food. You could never be too careful.
- **Radio DJ** - Haha! This is a joke. We had a very serious no-radio policy in the car. We were not going to spend all of that time listening to music when wonderful conversation could be had.

It was during our long road trips that the basis for our friendship was born. We would spend hours and hours talking about the problems of the world, Nick Collison, and our favorite brinners. Of course, we also talked about our bucket lists, Impossible Dreams and our verbs.

One of Kyle's Impossible Dreams was to purchase a house for his youth group. We brainstormed hundreds of ways how he could raise enough capital to buy a house. We came up with some brilliant ideas and these were some of our favorites.

- He could complete a massive walk-a-thon that lasted 10 years.

- He could sell a kidney on the black market. We did a ton of research on selling kidneys - we decided against it.

- He could consistently buy an S&P 500 low-cost index fund, preferably Vanguard, and buy the home outright at the age of 47.

Since none of those ideas were actually good ideas, Kyle came up with a different plan. He called it the *White Swan Project*.

The White Swan Project was simple. Kyle would take an ordinary piece of printing paper, fold it into an origami swan, and then trade it to someone for a better or more tradable item. He would then take that item and trade it for a better item, and then trade that item, and trade the next item, and then boom... **he would be a proud owner of the Kyle the Intern house!**

On one of our road trips Kyle came up with all of the steps necessary to start the *White Swan Project*. He found a piece of paper, learned how to fold an origami swan, and found the first ~~sucker~~ person willing to trade him something of value.

His first trade was a sensible trade. He had a friend from college who had an extra USB flash drive laying around that he was willing to part with for a White Origami Swan. **It was unclear if there was anything of value on the flash drive, but**

THAT WAS PART OF THE MYSTIC FOR THE NEXT TRADE.

Kyle then traded the flash drive (which contained all of the US national secrets) to a stranger for a karaoke machine. This is when I stepped in and tried to stop the *White Swan Project*. Kyle had achieved near optimal success. There is honestly no topping a karaoke machine. They are literally non-stop party machines. Kyle thought it was not as good as a house, and we disagreed, but it was his project so he continued.

He foolishly traded the karaoke machine for a television, and then traded the television for a TI-83 graphing calculator with ACT test prep. We seriously went from a karaoke machine to a graphing calculator. I am literally shaking my head as I write this sentence.

He then got stuck on the calculator and test prep for a few months.

Insert sarcastic voice

"Who would have ever thought that? I'm sure a graphing calculator is sooooo much better than a karaoke machine. I'm sure you can still trade the graphing calculator for a house. Go ahead and try!"

End sarcastic voice

---

* Worst trade in history.

Even though Kyle had a graphing calculator and some momentum, he still couldn't find anyone to trade him something of value. However, Kyle was not deterred. He did what any true-blooded American would do that was trying to trade from an origami swan to a house: he taped the calculator to his chest.

Kyle the Intern spent over two months of his freshman year of college walking around campus with a graphic calculator literally taped to his chest. He woke up every morning, got his packing tape, taped the calculator to his shirt, and bravely walked out onto campus.

He did this every day for **78 DAYS** until someone traded him a laptop for his dadgum calculator and ACT test prep.

He continued to trade items slowly and surely until he had an engagement ring with a fat one-carat diamond right on top of it. As of the writing of this book, Kyle is still attempting to trade up to a house. He has been offered commercial property, website design, and even a hand in marriage. He will not give up until he gets that house.

He had learned the Level Six lesson of *Live Your List*:

PARLAY.

Kyle hasn't finished the *White Swan Project* yet. It is one of his original bucket list items and it is currently his Impossible Dream. It helped him find his verb - develop. As you can imagine, someone as awesome as Kyle the Intern will not stop living his list when he finally obtains the *Kyle the Intern House*.

He still has several huge buckets on his list:

- Obtain his Masters in Electrical Engineering
- Graduate with his Ph.D.
- Travel to all seven continents by 40
- Watch every Oscar-winning *Best Picture* movie
- Run a marathon
- Complete a *New York Times* Crossword without any mistakes in ink
- Make a meal from scratch (raise the cow for the meat, plant the wheat for the buns, pasteurize the cheese)

You know that as soon as Kyle the Intern finishes all of these items, he will add more. He will finish one Impossible Dream and use the momentum from those experiences to parlay into another Impossible Dream.

THAT IS THE BEAUTY OF LIVING YOUR LIST.

You will be a continuous learner and choose to continue pursuing your verb.

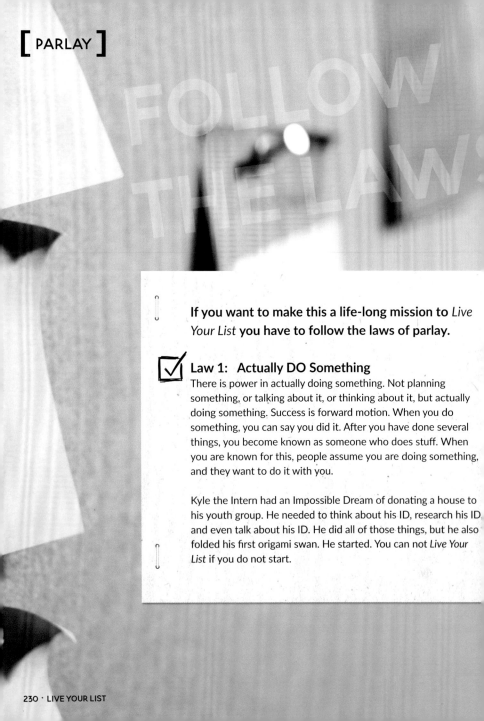

FOLLOW THE LAWS

If you want to make this a life-long mission to *Live Your List* you have to follow the laws of parlay.

☑ Law 1: Actually DO Something

There is power in actually doing something. Not planning something, or talking about it, or thinking about it, but actually doing something. Success is forward motion. When you do something, you can say you did it. After you have done several things, you become known as someone who does stuff. When you are known for this, people assume you are doing something, and they want to do it with you.

Kyle the Intern had an Impossible Dream of donating a house to his youth group. He needed to think about his ID, research his ID and even talk about his ID. He did all of those things, but he also folded his first origami swan. He started. You can not *Live Your List* if you do not start.

Law 2:   Forget the Perfect Plan
We love to plan. I know I do. I love whiteboards and charts. I love brainstorming and strategy sessions. But why do so many plans stop at just that - plans? Kyle had a great plan of trading a karaoke machine for a graphing calculator with ACT prep. It of course did not go according to plan, and Kyle had to improvise. He decided to tape that calculator to his chest until he found someone willing to trade with him.

Law 3:   Don't Be Lazy
Let's be honest, we love to be lazy. It is human nature to follow the path of least resistance. If you want to *Live Your List*, you know it requires hard work. You have to work towards a life of fulfillment through intentional living.

Kyle has not given up on his ID and will continue to strive for excellence through the rest of his life. Because of this he will end up traveling the world, making buckets of money, and maybe even someday get another karaoke machine.

Law 4: Meet People

We cannot take on this *Live Your List* journey alone. Impossible Dreams require collaboration from other music makers and dreamers of dreams. Find the people who are achieving the impossible and learn from them.

As a senior in high school, Kyle the Intern stepped outside of his comfort zone and went out of his way to attend our 20 Leadership Camp. During that camp, Kyle met his best friends, his future bosses, his co-workers, and potentially his future wife.* It was during the process of meeting people that Kyle changed the trajectory of his life.

* He would already have one if he kept the karaoke machine.

Law 5: Do Stuff With Those People

If anyone is going anywhere close to where you are going, jump on their bandwagon.

After his 20 Camp experience, Kyle the Intern took a chance and volunteered his services to Paradigm Shift as our first intern. He didn't know what he was exactly going to do, but he knew he wanted to be a part of the team. He now works for us full time and will someday be the boss.

Law 6: Don't Be Lazy

I felt this was worth repeating. You can not *Live Your List* unless you take personal responsibility, create a list, ACT on your Impossible Dream, chart your time, find your verb, and parlay your dreams.*

---

* I promise you I wasn't just repeating a law because I am lazy.

YOUR OWN ORIGAMI SWAN CHALLENGE

I would like for you to create your own Origami White Swan Project to try and parlay to your Impossible Dream. Find a piece of paper, fold it into an origami swan, and start to trade it to someone willing to help you achieve your dream.

You can share your progress in Kyle the Intern's White Swan Project Facebook group at *facebook.com/WhiteSwanProject*.

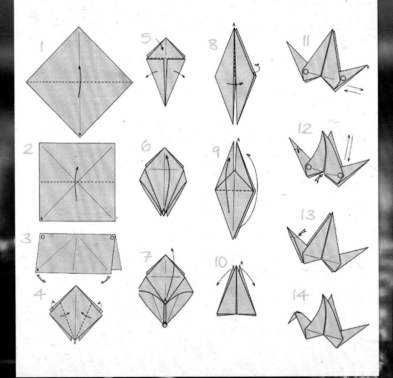

live
YOUR
list

MULTIPLY

Our first Paradigm Shift office had a toilet that leaked sewage into the yard. Not all of the time, but every few months our toilets would start to gurgle and we knew that it was time to call the plumber. Our office was an old yellow house in Muskogee, OK that we purchased for $20,000.

IT WAS NOT THE TAJ MAHAL.

Technically, it wasn't our first office. In the earliest years of Paradigm Shift Jerrod and I worked out of our homes. I worked in my home's spare bedroom and Jerrod worked at a coffee shop. The coffee shop wasn't really his home, but he was there enough that they gave him his own work space and named a coffee after him. Still today you can go to Jim & Em's Coffee Shop in Muskogee and get a "Hot Jerrod."

It was time for us to get a new office when my wife got pregnant and ~~selfishly~~ wanted to use our spare bedroom as a nursery for our newborn instead of an office/podcast studio for Paradigm Shift. We looked around Tulsa for office space and realized that we would need to create a second business just to pay rent. We even considered selling "Hot Jerrods" for a few minutes.

After a few more months of searching*, we found the best option was to buy a 1200 square-foot, 3-bedroom house in our hometown of Muskogee. It wasn't very special, didn't have a ton of charm, but it was cheap!

Those first few months in the office were genuinely fun, and I will never forget some of the early responsibilities we had in addition to our roles as facilitators and speakers. A few of our roles:

1. **RACCOON POOP COLLECTOR.** The attic had a family of raccoons that were making our office a home before we moved in. We hired a professional to remove the family, but he did not remove the raccoon poop. During the hot summer months we would start to smell it in different parts of the house and one of us had to get in the pitch-black attic and remove the poo. It was a several-month process.

2. **CAT WRANGLER.** There were a few stray cats around the office that were harder to catch than a Tim Wakefield errant pitch.** These cats were the definition of feral. They were feral felines but apparently not great raccoon catchers. It also took months to catch all of the cats and find them a proper home.

3. **SEWAGE ENGINEER.** Did we mention earlier that poo spilled into the yard? We will spare you the details on that story.

---

* We only had nine months to search because Kristin did not want to have a nursery/podcast studio/office.)

** That was a very specific sports joke that will make a few baseball fans in the Northeastern United States chuckle.

It was during this time that we built the foundation of success for Paradigm Shift. Each year we doubled in the amount of clients we served, the amount of events we facilitated, and the amount of money we made.

We went from being a team of two young, handsome, gorgeous, and beautiful Paradigm Shift facilitators to a team of 50. We went from a small home in rural Oklahoma to an 11,000 square foot warehouse that is a technological masterpiece.

We went from making next to zero dollars to making over a million in a few short years.

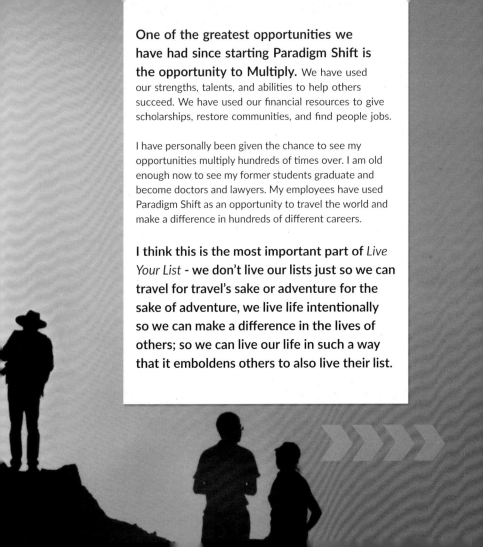

One of the greatest opportunities we have had since starting Paradigm Shift is the opportunity to Multiply. We have used our strengths, talents, and abilities to help others succeed. We have used our financial resources to give scholarships, restore communities, and find people jobs.

I have personally been given the chance to see my opportunities multiply hundreds of times over. I am old enough now to see my former students graduate and become doctors and lawyers. My employees have used Paradigm Shift as an opportunity to travel the world and make a difference in hundreds of different careers.

I think this is the most important part of *Live Your List* - we don't live our lists just so we can travel for travel's sake or adventure for the sake of adventure, we live life intentionally so we can make a difference in the lives of others; so we can live our life in such a way that it emboldens others to also live their list.

If you want to Multiply and leave a legacy for your world then you must mix the Three Ingredients of Legacy.

Ingredient 1: INTEGRITY

I once was a participant in a leadership workshop where the facilitator asked us to define integrity. Have you ever tried to define this word with a group of people? It means different things to each person in the group. Some think integrity means doing the right thing when no one is looking. Others say integrity is being devoutly committed to your personal morals or code. Some even describe it as intentionally pursuing pure thoughts about yourself and others.

Jerrod was sitting in this workshop with me, and he suggested that integrity might be a combination of these things. **Integrity is alignment of multiple things.**

IT IS A COMBINATION OF ALIGNING YOUR HEART, HEAD, AND HANDS.

HEART
HEAD
HANDS

HEART - Our belief system/core beliefs. These are the unshakable ideals that are concrete in your life. For some it is your Christian faith, for others it is your familial upbringing and the lessons you learned from your parents, and for others it is found through self-discovery. To find integrity in your life so you can Multiply, you must determine and outline your core belief system.

HEAD - Our thought patterns. I have consistently struggled with this one. Negative thoughts or insecurities have popped up from time to time as I have been traveling down my journey to live my list. I am not good enough. Others are better than me. People will think I am silly. It is important that we shape the thoughts that define our journey. This can be done with positive affirmations, reading, intentional conversations, or deep introspection. We need to make sure our thought patterns are consistent and in alignment with our belief system.

HANDS - Our actions. Zig Ziglar has an awesome quote that describes this part of integrity perfectly: "What you do speaks so loudly, I can not hear a word you are saying." If your core beliefs and thought patterns are not in alignment with your actions you will never Mulitply. I can not say I am a giving person and believe in giving without actually giving.

 All three of these ideals must be in alignment for us to have integrity in our lives.

[MULTIPLY]

Ingredient 2: DISCIPLINE

Discipline comes down to the root word disciple. Your
philosophy in life should determine your attitude,
your attitude will drive your actions, your actions will
determine your results, and your results will comprise
your lifestyle. This is what people see when they want
to follow you on your journey to *Live Your List*.

Ingredient 3: SACRIFICE

Lastly, if I want to Multiply, I must sacrifice. I must
sacrifice my ego - it's not about me. I have to sacrifice
credit - leaders take the blame and share the credit.
Sometimes I must sacrifice money, time, energy, or
short-term satisfaction to help others succeed.

I want to try an activity with you real quick. You will look silly doing it, so try to do it in public if possible. I want you to raise your hand as high as you can while seated. Make sure it is as high as it can go. Now, I want you to raise your hand two inches higher.

Were you able to raise it two inches higher?

OF COURSE YOU WERE.

If you have been reading the book this far you have successfully taken personal responsibility, you have written your lists, managed your time, set goals, found your verb, and parlayed. In essence you have raised your hand as high as you can.

If we want to Multiply (which is the ultimate level), we have to raise our hand an extra two inches. We have to give it a little more effort. We have to live a life of integrity, be disciplined, and sacrifice for others. If you are a compulsive list-checker be prepared to be disappointed... this is potentially a level we will never finish, because we may never arrive.

YOU WILL NEVER ARRIVE

Bill Gates lives his list. He may not know it yet, but he is an honorary Live Your Lister. I mean, just look at this guy's life.

At the age of 20 Bill dropped out of Harvard to co-found Microsoft with his lifelong friend Paul Allen. He became a billionaire by the age of 32 and the world's richest man by the time he was 40.

He was the chairman of one of the world's largest companies, lived in a mansion, could travel the world, and afford to do anything he wanted to do.

SO, WHAT DID HE DO?

LIVE YO

He stepped down from his daily responsibilities at Microsoft and started the Bill and Melinda Gates Foundation. They then announced the first round of Gates Millennium Scholars, part of a $1 billion effort to help 20,000 young people afford college over the next two decades (my sister and cousin were Gates Millennium Scholars).

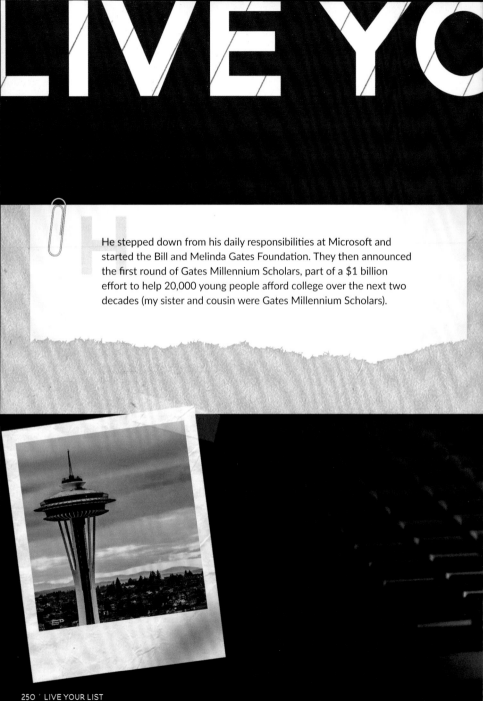

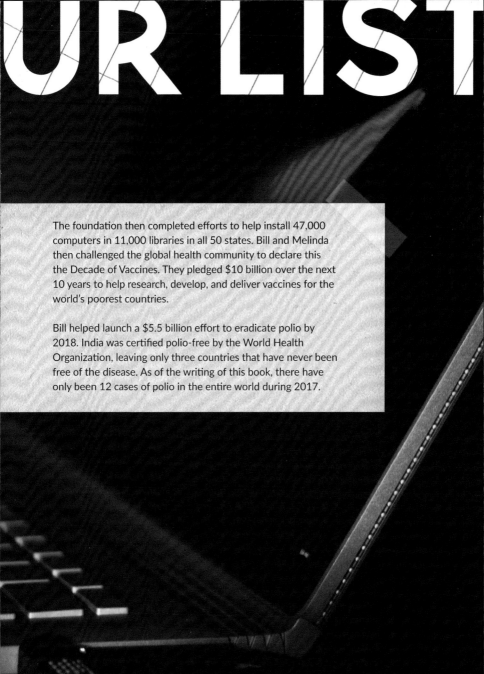

The foundation then completed efforts to help install 47,000 computers in 11,000 libraries in all 50 states. Bill and Melinda then challenged the global health community to declare this the Decade of Vaccines. They pledged $10 billion over the next 10 years to help research, develop, and deliver vaccines for the world's poorest countries.

Bill helped launch a $5.5 billion effort to eradicate polio by 2018. India was certified polio-free by the World Health Organization, leaving only three countries that have never been free of the disease. As of the writing of this book, there have only been 12 cases of polio in the entire world during 2017.

PASSION LED US

Bill Gates used his influence, time, resources, and money to Multiply his opportunities for other people. He parlayed his business success to achieve his Impossible Dream of eradicating disease. I am sure that if we were able to sit down and interview Bill Gates today*, he would tell us his life's work is far from being done. He never stopped reaching for more. He never stopped living his list.

* Believe me, we tried.

The good news is you do not have to be Bill Gates to *Live Your List*. Will I ever drop out of Harvard to start one of the world's largest companies? Doubtful. Will I ever be the world's richest man? Maybe. Bill isn't the only person on the planet that gets to live an amazing life! You can travel the world, learn new things, experience new cultures, and achieve huge dreams. You will do great things, not because you are special like Bill, but because you made a conscious decision to live an inspired life.

I think that is the biggest misconception about the *Live Your List* philosophy. People assume you must be rich, super intelligent, freakishly talented, or 100% carefree to *Live Your List*. All it takes is an everyday mentality to do more, be more, dream more. From here on out, every time you see Bill Gates I want you to know you are just as amazing as he is.

You have every opportunity to *Live Your List*...start living it today!

I DECIDED TO DO THIS WITH THE *LIVE YOUR LIST* PROJECT.

LIVE YOUR

In the fall of 2017, we started the *Live Your List Project*. Our goal was to help as many people as we could check items off of their bucket lists. For 86 consecutive days, we did just that. I am going to continue this project for the foreseeable future so that I can help Multiply and leave a legacy.

Some of the items were huge!
I helped my friend Rachel accomplish her bucket list item of going to Africa. I helped Jerrod ride an elephant. I even ran a half-marathon with Neha.

Some of the items were small.
I did a food challenge at the local hot dog stand with Roy. I watched a *Best Picture* winner with Kyle. I cut fruit with a samurai sword with Philip.

I also taught my daughter how to ride a bike, made jack-o-lanterns with my family, and traveled all over Muskogee.

The beauty of this challenge was not that I got to do amazing things - but it was that I got to do amazing things with amazing people. Those bonds and relationships will never be broken, and I am thankful for that opportunity.

THAT IS THE LEGACY
THAT I WANT TO LIVE.

My verb is to empower others. The *Live Your List* Project is the vehicle that is helping me travel down the road of life towards a life of fulfillment. I am empowering others to live the best life possible and to push them to maximize their strengths. I want to show people that they are meant for so much more than a normal life. They are meant to live a *Live Your List* life.

LIVE
YOUR
LIST
PROJECT

257

You may not be Bill Gates or even Ryan Eller, but if we stopped for a second to discuss your life, **what would be the legacy you would want to leave behind? When you are old and feeble on your deathbed, how would you want to be remembered?**

WHATEVER THE ANSWER MAY BE, LET'S INTENTIONALLY START LIVING A LIFE THAT REPRESENTS OUR FUTURE SELF.

I read of a man who stood to speak
at the funeral of a friend.
He referred to the dates on the tombstone
from the beginning...to the end.

He noted that first came the date of birth
and spoke the following date with tears,
but he said what mattered most of all
was the dash between those years.

For that dash represents all the time
that they spent alive on earth.
And now only those who loved them
know what that little line is worth.

For it matters not, how much we own,
the cars...the house...the cash.
What matters is how we live and love
and how we spend our dash.

So, think about this long and hard.
Are there things you'd like to change?
For you never know how much time is left
that can still be rearranged.

If we could just slow down enough
to consider what's true and real
and always try to understand
the way other people feel.

And be less quick to anger
and show appreciation more
and love the people in our lives
like we've never loved before.

If we treat each other with respect
and more often wear a smile,
remembering that this special dash
might only last a little while.

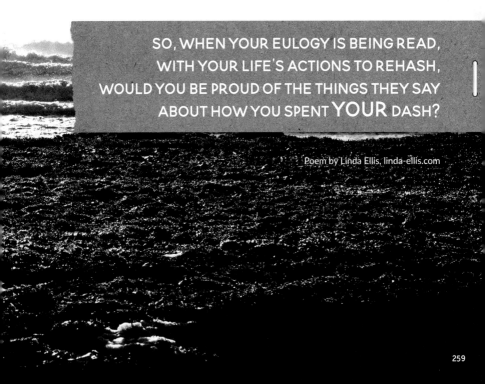

SO, WHEN YOUR EULOGY IS BEING READ,
WITH YOUR LIFE'S ACTIONS TO REHASH,
WOULD YOU BE PROUD OF THE THINGS THEY SAY
ABOUT HOW YOU SPENT YOUR DASH?

Poem by Linda Ellis, linda-ellis.com

What will be included in your dash? Who will go on that journey with you? Will you be proud of the years you spend on this earth?

Answer the questions below to help you determine what your legacy will be as you Multiply and *Live Your List*.

_____

_____

_____

_____

_____

_____

_____

_____

_____

_____

_____

_____

_____

_____

_____

_____

_____

_____

_____

_____

_____

_____

_____

_____

What is your verb?

_____

_____

What vehicles are you currently using to help you fulfill your purpose?

_____

_____

What is your Impossible Dream?

_____

_____

How will you ACT on your ID?

_____

_____

How can you Parlay your IDs to accomplish even bigger IDs?

_____

_____

If you died tomorrow, what words would you want people to use to describe your life?

_____

_____

Who are some people you can help live their list?

_____

_____

What would you do with those people?

_____

_____

How can you use your opportunities to give back to your school, work, community, or family?

_____

_____

What are three things you can do right now to help define your future legacy?

_____

_____

If you *Live Your List* you are taking control of your destiny. I certainly have. I went from being a small town son of a dairy farmer to a world traveling business owner. If you *Live Your List* you will live an inspired life full of adventure and intrigue as a life-long learner.

If you have read this entire book then I know you will do great things with your life. I know you will find your purpose and wisely use the time you have on this earth.

"Our deepest fear is not that we are inadequate.
Our deepest fear is that we are powerful beyond measure.
It is our light, not our darkness that most frightens us.
We ask ourselves, Who am I to be brilliant,
gorgeous, talented, fabulous?
Actually, who are you not to be?
You are a child of God.
Your playing small does not serve the world.
There is nothing enlightened about shrinking
so that other people won't feel insecure around you.
We are all meant to shine, as children do.
We were born to make manifest the glory of God that is within us.
It's not just in some of us; it's in everyone.
And as we let our own light shine, we unconsciously
give other people permission to do the same.
As we are liberated from our own fear,
our presence automatically liberates others."

— *Marianne Williamson*

My challenge to you is to use the opportunities you have been given in life to help others live their list. **Make a difference in your world. Plant that tree, fund that scholarship, help someone succeed.** That is when you will truly be Living Your List.

live YOUR list

RESOURCES

WHATEVER
IT
TAKES

1,001 BUCKET LIST ITEMS BY CATEGORY

ADVENTURE

1. Air Boat Across an Alligator Infested Swamp
2. Arrive By Seaplane to a remote location
3. Attempt to ice climb over a glacier
4. Bamboo raft down a mystical river
5. BASE jump off of a tall building
6. Bathe an Elephant
7. Bathe in a hot spring with strangers
8. Bathe in milk
9. Be a passenger on a train
10. Be a seat filler at the Oscars
11. Be a tourist in your own town and go somewhere you've never been but always wanted to go
12. Be in the delivery room during childbirth
13. Be one of the few to go to the top of the Seven Summits
14. Be one of the first humans to travel to space
15. Bet on a horse at the horse races
16. Bid on an auction item at Christie's or Sotheby's
17. Boogie board in the ocean over some mighty waves
18. Bungee jump off of a bridge
19. Bury a time capsule and open it years later
20. Buy a really stupid novelty item from eBay and give it to a friend
21. Buy a ticket for a random flight at the airport
22. Canoe down a river
23. Catch a lightning bug and place it in a jar
24. Catch a ride in a rickshaw
25. Catch a snipe while snipe hunting
26. Celebrate a White Christmas
27. Celebrate your birthday in a different country
28. Cheer the host at a live taping of a late night show
29. Climb to the top of a tree and swing from the highest branches
30. Complete any 90-day challenge
31. Connect with nature while primitive camping
32. Conquer a fear
33. Convince some friends to go cow tipping
34. Cross the country in a private jet
35. Deactivate all social media for a week
36. Design a homemade river raft - then go rafting
37. Dirty yourself up with a mud bath
38. Discover a pearl in an oyster
39. Dive into a polar plunge in a cold-water environment
40. Dive to the depths of the ocean to see the Titanic
41. Do a backflip on a pogo stick
42. Do donuts while off-roading
43. Drive a Zamboni
44. Drive a tank
45. Drive across Route 66
46. Drive an 18-wheeler
47. Drive as fast as your can go in a Ferrari
48. Drive through every county in your state
49. Dry off by campfire
50. Eat fire
51. Experience zero gravity
52. Explore a cave while spelunking
53. Extract honey from a beehive
54. Feed a koala bear
55. Find treasure with a metal detector
56. Find your way through a labyrinth
57. Fly a kite on a windy day
58. Fly a plane across the sky
59. Fly at the speed of sound
60. Fly internationally on a double decker plane
61. Fly over a city on a helicopter
62. Freeze yourself during cryotherapy
63. Gaze at the stars in a glass igloo
64. Get a book signed by your favorite author
65. Get a fish pedicure
66. Get a professional massage
67. Get a tattoo with a friend
68. Get into a situation to need a translator
69. Get spoiled in first class
70. Glide over the hills in a gyrocopter
71. Go hang gliding in a remote location
72. Go streaking
73. Go to a ceremony of a religion that is not your own
74. Haggle at an open market
75. Hang onto a rope while rock climbing
76. Have your fortune read by a fortune teller
77. Hold a shark
78. Hold a tarantula sized spider
79. Hold onto a dolphin fin as it carries you through the ocean
80. Hug a redwood
81. Hunt for wild mushrooms
82. Hunt small prey at a falconry class

83. Indoor Skydive
84. Jump into a pile of leaves
85. Jump into a pool full of jello
86. Jump into a pool fully clothed
87. Jump off a cliff
88. Jump out of a helicopter onto a mountain while heli-skiing
89. Karate chop and break a board
90. Kiss someone in the rain
91. Land a flip on a wakeboard
92. Last eight seconds while you ride a bull
93. Leave your stress in a sensory deprivation tank
94. Let someone read your palm
95. Live in a different country
96. Live in a houseboat
97. Live one month without spending money on anything other than necessities
98. Look out for criminals on a police ride-along
99. Luge down a huge hill
100. Meander through a bamboo forest
101. Meditate on the side of a mountain
102. Meet a world leader
103. Meet an animal who is internet famous
104. Meet someone famous randomly
105. Milk a cow
106. Name a star
107. Navigate a boat down a river
108. Navigate a personal underwater sub
109. Navigate a segway
110. Observe a bear in the wild
111. Obtain backstage passes to a concert
112. Officiate a wedding
113. Organize a picnic outing
114. Own a Chanel suit
115. Own a Louis Vuitton purse
116. Own a Rolex
117. Own a Rolls Royce, an Aston Martin, or a Bentley
118. Own a beach house
119. Own a house with a fireplace
120. Own a pet monkey
121. Own a private jet
122. Own a professional football team
123. Own a successful business
124. Own an Armani suit
125. Own an island
126. Pan for gold
127. Parachute out of a cargo plane
128. Partake in a food fight
129. Participate in a protest
130. Participate in a sweat lodge ceremony

131. Participate in an Indian Wedding
132. Participate in a cattle drive
133. Pay off a stranger's Christmas layaway
134. Pet a bear cub
135. Pet a dolphin
136. Pet a lion cub
137. Pet a penguin
138. Pierce your ears with a friend
139. Pitch a tent in your backyard
140. Plant a flag on top of a mountain
141. Plant your own garden
142. Pose with a figure at a wax museum
143. Proudly walk around at a nudist colony
144. Race a car on a NASCAR track
145. Race some friends while four-wheeling on sand dunes
146. Raise your hands in the air on the ten largest roller coasters in the world
147. Reach for the earth while tandem skydiving
148. Receive acupuncture
149. Record a meteor shower
150. Record a music video
151. Relax in a natural hot spring
152. Relax in a salt water tank
153. Renovate a mansion
154. Research the history of your favorite sports team
155. Restore an old classic car
156. Ride a jet ski
157. Ride a motorcycle
158. Ride a unicycle
159. Ride an ostrich
160. Rise above the water while Flyboarding in a Water Jet Pack
161. Roll a somersault down a hill
162. Rollerblade with friends
163. Rope a cow at a dude ranch
164. Run for political office
165. Sing at a concert to an artist you're not familiar with
166. Sail a boat
167. Scare someone at a haunted house
168. Score an autograph from your favorite celebrity
169. Scuba dive
170. Send a fan letter to your favorite celebrity
171. Send a message in a bottle and get a response
172. Send a Slinky down an escalator
173. Set a Guinness World Record
174. Shake hands with a president, current or former
175. Shake hands with your favorite celebrity
176. Share your most embarrassing moment
177. Shear a sheep
178. Shoot a machine gun

179. Shop on Rodeo Drive	228. Take English riding lessons
180. Shuck oysters	229. Take a Sunday drive in a convertible with the top down
181. Sit front row at a fashion show	230. Take a friend on a spontaneous road trip
182. Sit on a jury	231. Take a natural mud bath
183. Sit on the front row of a concert	232. Take a picture of the colors of the Northern Lights
184. Skateboard at a skating park	233. Take a punch from Mike Tyson
185. Skeet shoot	234. Take a ride on an elephant
186. Ski a black diamond trail	235. Take a road trip by yourself
187. Ski down the side of a mountain	236. Take a seat on the world's largest Ferris Wheel
188. Skinny dip with strangers	237. Take a vacation with no itinerary
189. Skydive	238. Take in the sunrise and sunset in the same day
190. Sleep in a hostel with strangers	239. Take it easy on an aimless drive
191. Sleep in a yurt	240. Teach English in a foreign country
192. Sleep in an overnight train	241. Teach a parrot to talk
193. Sleep on a trampoline	242. Team up with someone and ride a tandem bicycle
194. Sleep on the beach	243. Throw a boomerang and receive it in the same throw
195. Slide down a firehouse pole	244. Throw a dart at a map and go to that spot
196. Smoke a fine cigar	245. Throw poo with a monkey
197. Smoke a hookah	246. Touch a giant cactus
198. Snowshoe across an unknown mountain path	247. Touch a stingray
199. Spend $10,000 during a care-free shopping spree	248. Tour a city in a horse and carriage
200. Spend New Year's Eve in an exotic location	249. Train a dog to do tricks
201. Spend a day without speaking	250. Travel across the sky in a blimp
202. Spend a night in a haunted house	251. Travel back in time at an Amish community
203. Spend a night in a tree house	252. Travel for one month straight with only a backpack
204. Spend a week at a 5-star spa	253. Travel to space in a spacecraft
205. Spend a weekend at the world's most expensive hotel	254. Trek across a frozen river without fear
206. Spin a basketball on your finger	255. Try Chinese cupping
207. Spoil yourself at a 5-star hotel	256. Try to catch a fish while Snubadiving
208. Stand face to face with a monk at a monastery	257. Try to catch the end of a rainbow
209. Stand next to someone who is over seven feet tall	258. Try to see a whale while paragliding
210. Stand on a glacier	259. Use a paddle to bid at an auction
211. Stand on the floor of a drilling rig	260. Use a tractor to till the Earth
212. Stand under a waterfall	261. Use your binoculars to find whales while whale watching
213. Stand up paddle board	262. Vacation solo
214. Star in a commercial	263. Visit a butterfly house
215. Start a band	264. Visit a temple
216. Start a business	265. Walk a cheetah
217. Start a hobby with a stranger	266. Walk around for a day in middle eastern attire
218. Stay awake for 24 hours	267. Walk everywhere for a week
219. Step out and become a foreign exchange student	268. Walk on hot coals
220. Stick your head out of the sunroof in a limo	269. Walk on stilts
221. Stomp on grapes to make wine	270. Walk through a rainforest with a machete
222. Successfully complete a heist	271. Walk with a lion
223. Survive a day without seeing	272. Watch a movie at a drive-in movie theater
224. Survive the rapids while white water rafting	273. Watch the launch of a space shuttle
225. Swim with sea turtles	274. Watch the ocean go by on a cruise ship
226. Swing above the crowd in a trapeze class	275. Watch the sun rise on the top of a water tower
227. Swing around at a ballroom dance class	276. Wear an extravagant mask to a masquerade ball

277. Wear colored contact lenses
278. Wear your birthday suit to a nude beach
279. Win a Gold Medal
280. Win a game of Ping Pong
281. Win a game show
282. Win a giveaway prize off of the radio
283. Win a lucky draw
284. Win a stuffed animal at a fair
285. Win big at an Indian Casino
286. Win the lottery
287. Witness a meteor shower
288. Witness total solar eclipse
289. Wrap a snake around your neck
290. Yell Bingo! At a Bingo Hall

CREATIVE

291. Act in a film (homemade or big-budget)
292. Act in a play at a local theater
293. Apply for a reality TV Show
294. Attend a Jewish Wedding and dance the horah
295. Attend a music festival and dance with the people
296. Attend a native American Pow-Wow
297. Be a dancer in a flash mob
298. Be a groupie for your favorite band
299. Be a mascot for something
300. Be an extra on a TV show
301. Be in a band
302. Build a village around a model train while wearing an engineering outfit
303. Build a sandcastle on the beach
304. Build an igloo in a cold-weather country
305. Bust a fire from wood
306. Complete a 1000-piece jigsaw puzzle
307. Compose a song for a professional singer
308. Crochet a gift for someone
309. Dance everywhere you go for a day
310. Dance on top of a bar
311. Dance or sing with Miss America
312. Deliver a speech to over 10,000 people
313. Draw a Zentangle
314. Enter a pageant you are not qualified to win
315. Fall in the snow and make a snow angel
316. Feel yourself being hypnotized
317. Figure out how many licks it actually takes to get to the tootsie roll center of a Tootsie Pop
318. Fold an origami swan
319. Give a commencement speech
320. Give a wedding speech as a best man or maid of honor
321. Grow a seed
322. Grow Bonsai Trees
323. Grow prize-winning roses
324. Have a James Bond movie marathon
325. Have an article of clothing made for you
326. Have your picture taken for the newspaper
327. Have your portrait painted
328. Hire a celebrity to sing at your birthday party
329. Hire a personal shopper
330. Hone your negotiation skills
331. Host a cocktail party
332. Keep a greenhouse
333. Keep bees alive as a beekeeper
334. Knead a clay pot
335. Knit a scarf
336. List your top 100 favorite songs
337. Live 24 hours screen free
338. Make a Tye-Dye Shirt
339. Make a balloon animal
340. Master a freestanding handstand
341. Create a secret handshake with someone and never tell a soul
342. Figure out how you would survive without electricity
343. Own a collection
344. Paint something to hang in your home
345. Partake in a renaissance fair
346. Participate in a poetry reading
347. Participate in dinner theater
348. Perform a card trick for a large audience
349. Perform a public presentation
350. Perform stand up comedy at a comedy club
351. Photograph an endangered species
352. Pose for a professional photo shoot
353. Publish your own book
354. Sell a piece of your artwork
355. Sell clothes from your personal clothing line
356. Send a handwritten note every day for a year
357. Sing to an audience
358. Sing with a music legend in concert
359. Sing your favorite song at a karaoke bar
360. Solve a Rubik's cube
361. Start an art collection
362. Submit a joke for Laffy Taffy
363. Surprise someone with a complete makeover
364. Watch all Golden Globe Best Pictures with a friend who loves movies
365. Watch and rank all the best Oscar films
366. Write a poem
367. Write to a pen pal

EDUCATIONAL / PROFESSIONAL

368. Apply for a Commercial Driver's License
369. Ask for a raise or a promotion
370. Attend your 10-year high school reunion
371. Author a children's book
372. Be chosen to give a TED talk
373. Be completely debt free
374. Be interviewed for the TV news
375. Be the boss
376. Become a billionaire (and then give away your fortunes)
377. Become a member of an exclusive club
378. Become a self-made millionaire
379. Camp with your family in a remote location
380. Celebrate your 50th Wedding Anniversary with the love of your life
381. Create a YouTube channel (even if you have no subscribers)
382. Develop a source of passive income
383. Donate $1 million to charity
384. Donate money to a relief organization
385. Donate to the Red Cross
386. Dress to the 9's every day for a week
387. Earn your GED
388. Earn your a PhD
389. Establish a foundation to give away your money
390. Flip a house and sell it for profit
391. Get accepted into Harvard (or some other Ivy League School)
392. Get featured in the media for something you are proud of
393. Graduate college with your dream degree
394. Graduate high school
395. Graduate with a 4.0
396. Graduate with a Master's degree
397. Graduate with honors
398. Have a social media post go viral
399. Have one of your photographs published in a magazine
400. Invent something
401. Mentor another person
402. Never miss a day of class
403. Open a franchise
404. Organize a fundraiser
405. Receive an honorary degree from a credible university
406. Set up a non-profit & raise money for a cause you believe in
407. Start a podcast
408. Work a profession in a different field
409. Write a blog

FAMILY

410. Adopt a child
411. Adopt a pet from a rescue mission
412. Be a foster parent for kids with no home
413. Build doll houses for your child
414. Build your dream house for your family
415. Build a treehouse for my kids
416. Buy your mom her dream car
417. Coach your son's little league team
418. Create a coat of arms for your family
419. Create a home with an inviting, joyous, comfortable, loving atmosphere
420. Create family rituals and traditions to celebrate holidays and important life events
421. Decorate a Christmas tree in every room of your house with your family
422. Draw out your Family Tree
423. Figure out your family's history
424. Get a tattoo ring with the love of your life
425. Get married to the love of your life
426. Give birth to a child
427. Give your daughter away at her wedding
428. Handmake all family Christmas gifts one year
429. Hold at least one of your great-grandchildren
430. Host a foreign exchange student
431. Host a holiday event
432. Host a non-American for Thanksgiving
433. Learn your family ancestry
434. Meet the love of your life
435. Pass on a family heirloom to your child
436. Plan an elaborate surprise for someone you love
437. Play with your grandchildren
438. Prepare a will
439. Raise a happy and healthy child
440. Reconnect with a lost loved one
441. Reconnect with your most influential teachers and thank them
442. Renew your wedding vows after being married for ten years
443. Ride a horse on the beach with someone you love
444. Send a love letter
445. Sled down a snow-covered hill with your kids
446. Spoil your grandchildren
447. Start a tradition of getting together with your extended family for a barbecue once a year
448. Stay married to the same person for as long as you both live
449. Surprise your parents with a dream vacation
450. Take your significant other to visit your childhood home

451. Witness and be present at significant moments of your child's life
452. Write a letter to each of your children telling them what you want them to know about your life and the lessons you've learned
453. Write a letter to your future self

FOOD

454. Attend a pig roast (bonus points if the pig is roasted with an apple in its mouth)
455. Attend a proper British afternoon tea in London
456. Be a vegetarian for a month
457. Buy food from a food truck
458. Buy 99 cent pizza in NYC
459. Compete in a food challenge
460. Cook every dish in a cookbook
461. Create a meal completely from scratch
462. Dip fancy foods in fondue
463. Drink a beer at Oktoberfest
464. Drink a beer in the Netherlands
465. Drink a bottle of champagne that costs over $1,000.00
466. Drink a glass of wine in Lyon, France
467. Drink juice from a fresh coconut on a tropical island
468. Drink a martini at an ice bar
469. Drink Sake in Japan
470. Drink vodka in Russia
471. Eat a bowl of chowder in New England
472. Eat a deep fried Twinkie at the fair
473. Eat a Maine lobster
474. Eat a Philly Cheesesteak in Philadelphia
475. Eat a shark in Iceland
476. Eat an insect in a foreign country
477. Eat at a Brazilian steakhouse in Brazil
478. Eat Belgium waffles in Belgium
479. Eat buffalo wings in Buffalo
480. Eat fancy food in Paris
481. Eat fish and chips in England
482. Eat guinea pig in Peru
483. Eat frog legs in the Deep South
484. Eat octopus next to the ocean
485. Eat ox balls in Kenya
486. Fillet a fish that you caught
487. Go a week without eating
488. Go wine tasting in Napa Valley
489. Have someone serve your breakfast in bed
490. Order fried caterpillar in Africa
491. Order one of everything on a menu
492. Order room service

493. Savor your pasta in Italy
494. Try all of the food and drink at an all-inclusive resort
495. Try different types of pizza in Chicago
496. Try every flavor of ice cream at an ice cream shoppe
497. Try food from a world-class chef
498. Try Whale in Alaska
499. Use chopsticks to eat sushi in Tokyo

LEARN

500. Bake a loaf of bread from scratch
501. Be able to recite all 50 state capitals from memory
502. Be an apprentice to a skilled worker
503. Become a Cheese Connoisseur
504. Become a Wine Connoisseur
505. Become the premiere expert on one major artist
506. Bench press your weight
507. Brew your own butter beer
508. Build a Little Free Library
509. Build something with your own hands
510. Build your own website
511. Construct furniture from scratch
512. Cook a fancy dish at a gourmet cooking class
513. Create Mandalas
514. Create a cookbook
515. Culture yourself during a social etiquette class
516. DIY something for your home and proudly display it
517. Discover a favorite author and know why he/she is your favorite
518. Draw yourself at a drawing class
519. Fill a small library with high quality books
520. Give mouth to mouth to a mannequin during a first aid course
521. Join a book club
522. Keep a daily journal for a year
523. Learn to braid hair
524. Learn a form of martial arts
525. Learn a full yoga routine
526. Learn a latin dance
527. Learn a line dance
528. Learn a musical instrument
529. Learn a new word every day for a year
530. Learn a traditional dance
531. Learn about investing
532. Learn all of the countries in the world
533. Learn all of the presidents in order
534. Learn different handshakes from around the world
535. Learn glassblowing
536. Learn how to change a tire

537. Learn how to change your oil
538. Learn how to code
539. Learn how to cook your favorite meal
540. Learn how to cut hair
541. Learn how to do a backflip
542. Learn how to do fancy makeup
543. Learn how to do your taxes
544. Learn how to drive a motorcycle
545. Learn how to drive a stick shift
546. Learn how to hem a pair of pants
547. Learn to make make sushi
548. Learn how to pick a lock
549. Learn how to pitch a tent
550. Learn how to play a new sport
551. Learn how to play a song on the piano
552. Learn how to play backgammon
553. Learn how to play poker
554. Learn how to properly set a table
555. Learn how to read a map
556. Learn how to read braille
557. Learn how to say the alphabet backwards
558. Learn how to say hello in ten different languages
559. Learn how to shoot a bow and arrow
560. Learn how to shoot a gun
561. Learn how to swim
562. Learn how to use a power tool
563. Learn how to use chopsticks
564. Learn morse code
565. Learn sign language
566. Learn stress management
567. Learn the names of all of your close neighbors
568. Learn to bartend
569. Learn to brew beer
570. Learn to budget
571. Learn to compost your food waste
572. Learn to cook a fancy meal
573. Learn to do a cartwheel
574. Learn to do a wheelie on a bike
575. Learn to hula hoop
576. Learn to juggle
577. Learn to make candles
578. Learn to paint
579. Learn to play chess
580. Learn to read music
581. Learn to sculpt
582. Learn to sing
583. Learn to speak a foreign language
584. Learn to tie a bow tie
585. Learn to walk on your hands
586. Learn to write with both hands
587. Learn to yodel
588. Make a list of 100 books you want to read
589. Make homemade ice cream
590. Make models of cars, ships or airplanes
591. Make stained glass windows
592. Memorize the constellations
593. Memorize your favorite poem
594. Pass your driver's license test
595. Read a book a week for a year
596. Read a book about a subject you know nothing about
597. Read a book before the movie
598. Read all of Agatha Christie's mystery novels
599. Read all of Honoré de Balzac"s short stories and novels
600. Read all of the Harry Potter books
601. Read all of the Russian classics
602. Read all of the Sherlock Holmes mysteries
603. Read every book your favorite author has written
604. Read every novel that has won a Pulitzer Prize in the Fiction Category
605. Read every day for a year
606. Read ten books written by winners of the Nobel Prize in Literature
607. Read the Bible from cover to cover
608. Read the complete works of Shakespeare
609. Read the top 100 books of all time
610. Straighten out your life with a life coach
611. Study a different religion
612. Study cartography

PHYSICAL

613. Be able to bench-press 150 lbs
614. Be able to do 10 pull-ups
615. Be able to do 50 push-ups
616. Catch a fish while deep sea fishing
617. Catch a fish while ice fishing
618. Catch a foul ball at a MLB game
619. Charter a yacht
620. Climb a rope in a gym class
621. Compete in a bodybuilding competition
622. Compete in a fitness competition
623. Compete in an Ironman competition
624. Cycle across your state
625. Finish a triathlon
626. Perform the splits
627. Protect yourself during a self-defense class
628. Run a marathon
629. Run barefoot

630. Run the Boston Marathon
631. Shake it during a Zumba class
632. Show off your six-pack abs
633. Start a local running group
634. Work out until you have buns of steel

SPORTS

635. Attend a Final Four basketball game
636. Attend a Premiere League football match
637. Attend a rodeo and try your hand at roping
638. Attend the NBA All-Star Game
639. Be featured on the jumbotron at a professional sporting event
640. Bowl a perfect game
641. Carve a new path while snowboarding
642. Cheer for the opposing team in the home stands
643. Dunk a basketball
644. Golf at a private golf course
645. Hit a hole in one
646. Hit an archery bullseye
647. Hit the bullseye on a dart board
648. Hold on for dear life while windsurfing
649. Join a bowling league
650. Play a game of paintball
651. Play frisbee golf
652. Root for your team at a World Series game
653. Sit on the sidelines of a professional sporting event
654. Throw out the 1st pitch at an MLB game
655. Watch the NFL Pro Bowl
656. Watch the Yankees play the Red Sox at Fenway Park and Yankee Stadium
657. Watch the opening ceremonies for the Summer Olympics
658. Watch your favorite sport at the Winter Olympics
659. Wear a fun hat at the Kentucky Derby
660. Wear a soccer uniform at a World Cup Match in Brazil
661. Witness at a sumo wrestling match in Japan

TRAVEL
Africa

662. Carefully dive with crocodiles in Africa
663. Carve your name in a tree at the Cape of Good Hope
664. Climb Mount Kilimanjaro in Tanzania
665. Cross the water to Zanzibar
666. Cruise the Nile River
667. Explore the Atlas Mountains of Morocco
668. Gaze upon a giraffe in Nairobi, Kenya

669. Guess the age of a large tree in Madagascar
670. Raft down the Zambezi
671. See African animals on a wildlife safari
672. Sleep under the stars in the Sahara
673. Stand next to the pyramids in Giza
674. Stare into the Ngorongoro Crater in Tanzania
675. Stroll along the beaches in Cape Town, South Africa
676. Stroll through the Sagano Bamboo Forest in Japan
677. Stroll with the Kalahari Bushmen
678. Swim in Devil's Pool at Victoria Falls in Zambia
679. Swim with sharks in Cape Town
680. Visit the Sossusvlei Dunes in Namibia
681. Walk with a black rhino in Namibia
682. Watch the Indian and Atlantic ocean meet
683. Watch the Serengeti in Tanzania

Asia

684. Act like a spy at the Kremlin in Russia
685. Admire the Shwedagon Pagoda in Rangoon, Burma
686. Attempt to ride a train in India
687. Be awestruck by the terra-cotta warriors of Xi'an
688. Behold Bagan in Myanmar
689. Brave the climb to the Tiger's Nest, Taktsang Palphug
690. Capture the beauty of the temples and gardens of Kyoto
691. Cruise in Ha Long Bay, Vietnam
692. Dune Buggy on the way to an Arabian Camp
693. Experience Istanbul's Call to Prayer
694. Explore the ancient ruins of Petra in Jordan
695. Face the Lion's Rock at the ancient royal compound of Sigiriya in Sri Lanka
696. Feel the awe of history in the Buddhist cave temples of Dambulla
697. Find yourself lost in a crowd in Tokyo
698. Float in the Dead Sea
699. Follow Jesus' paths in Jerusalem
700. Follow in the emperor's footsteps in Beijing's Forbidden City
701. Get a henna tattoo in India
702. Go vertical caving in Yogyakarta, Indonesia
703. Hike Mount Fuji in Japan
704. Hike the Caucasus in Georgia
705. Hike to base camp at Mt. Everest
706. Hold on for dear life at the Walk of Faith in Tianmen Mountain
707. Hot air balloon ride in Cappadocia (Turkey)
708. Hunt with eagles in Mongolia
709. Light a yak-butter candle for fertility at Chimi Lakhang

710. Live lavishly at Durrat Al Bahrain, the horseshoe and fish-shaped islands that lie off the South coast of Bahrain
711. Marvel at the temples at Wadi Rum in Southern Jordan
712. Participate in the color festival (Holi) in India
713. Pay the fee to visit Bhutan
714. Pick a bloom off of a cherry blossom in Japan
715. Purify yourself in the Ganges in India
716. Receive a jukai blessing at the Garan complex in Kyosan
717. Release a candle at Yi Peng Festival in Thailand
718. Revisit history in Turkey
719. Ride the elevator to top of the Burj Khalifa in Dubai
720. Salute the sun at Bhangarh in India
721. See the sights along the Transiberian Railway
722. See the view of Hong Kong from Victoria Peak
723. See yourself in the House of Mirrors in Kuwait City
724. Shop for souvenirs in Istanbul
725. Stand atop the Petronas Twin Towers in Malaysia
726. Stand in front of the Taj Mahal
727. Stand in the center of the Islamic world at Mecca
728. Taste the olive oil in Jerusalem
729. Trek across the Himalayas
730. Visit a Mosque in Saudi Arabia
731. Visit the Old Silk Road
732. Walk along the Abraham Path following in the footsteps of the prophet Abraham 4,000 years ago
733. Walk around Singapore's sky gardens
734. Walk the Great Wall of China
735. Watch camel racing in Qatar
736. Watch the sunset from Wat Phrathat, Chiang Mai's holiest shrine
737. Watch the whirling dervishes in Istanbul

Europe

738. Attend Fashion Week at one of the fashion capitals of the world - London, LA, NYC, Rome, Milan, Barcelona, Berlin
739. Attend mass at Notre Dame Cathedral in Paris
740. Become a child again at Tivoli Gardens in Copenhagen
741. Breathe in the lavender fields in Provence, France
742. Catch a flamenco show in Andalusia, Spain
743. Celebrate St. Patrick's Day in Ireland
744. Chase waterfalls in Bosnia-Herzegovina
745. Cheer on the cyclists at the Tour de France
746. Chime with the clock at Big Ben in London
747. Climb Leukerbad Via Ferrata in Switzerland
748. Climb Skellig Islands off of the coast of Ireland
749. Cross Europe on the Orient Express
750. Cross the Straits of Gibraltar on a ferry
751. Dogsled in Finland
752. Drive as fast as you can on the Autobahn in Germany
753. Explore the Lascaux Caves in southwestern France
754. Explore the charming streets of Edinburgh, Scotland
755. Feel like a giant at Madurodam in the Netherlands
756. Find viking ruins on the Faroe Islands
757. Gamble at Monte Carlo in Monaco
758. Geek out at Trinity College
759. Get a picture walking across Abbey Road in London
760. Go island hopping in Greece
761. Heat up in a sauna in Norway
762. High five someone at the Leaning Tower of Pisa, Italy
763. Hike to the top of Arthur's Seat in Edinburgh
764. Imagine life in ancient Pompeii
765. Jog in the Luxembourg Gardens
766. Kiss the Blarney stone in Ireland
767. Look over London from the the London Eye
768. Make a wish at the Trevi Fountain, Rome
769. Make your way through the canals of Amsterdam
770. Marvel at St. Peter's Basilica
771. Marvel at the history of Athens, Greece
772. Marvel at the history of the Parthenon in Greece
773. Observe the changing of the guard at Buckingham Palace
774. Paint the views at Cinque Terre, Italy
775. Peer over the Cliffs of Moher in Ireland
776. Play golf in Scotland
777. Pray to the gods at Stonehenge
778. Pretend to be knighted at a castle in Germany
779. Recite the Apostle's Creed at Vatican City
780. Relax on the uncrowded beaches of Montenegro
781. Remember what you learned in history class while walking around the coliseum in Rome
782. Rent a villa in Tuscany for the summer
783. Ride a ride at Disney World in a different country
784. Ring a bell at the Notre Dame Cathedral
785. Row around Lake Bled in Slovenia
786. Run with the bulls in Pampalona, Spain
787. Sail around the Greek Isles
788. Say a prayer at the Alhambra in Spain
789. Search for Nessie at Loch Ness in Scotland
790. Shop at Harrods, London
791. Sing a song in a gondola in Venice
792. Sit on top of a double decker bus in London
793. Ski the Swiss Alps
794. Sleep at an ice hotel in Sweden
795. Soak in a thermal bath in Budapest
796. Somehow make a guard laugh at Buckingham Palace
797. Spook someone at the Catacombs in Paris
798. Stand beneath the Eiffel Tower at night
799. Stand in Red Square, Moscow

800. Stand in front of the Mona Lisa at the Louvre in Paris
801. Stand next to Michelangelo's David
802. Stay at a Bed and Breakfast at Claude Monet's garden at Giverny
803. Stretch your neck at the Sistine Chapel
804. Stroll the Charles Bridge at dawn in silence
805. Study history in ancient Greece
806. Swim in the Blue Lagoon in Iceland
807. Take a canal tour in Amsterdam
808. Touch the white walls of Santorini
809. Tour Acropolis in Greece
810. Tour a windmill in Holland
811. Tour the Northeastern Fjords in Iceland
812. Travel on the tube from London to Paris
813. View all of the sights on Iceland's Ring Road
814. Visit a Concentration Camp in Germany
815. Visit every capital city in Europe
816. Visit the Caves of Altamira near Santilliana del Mar in Cantabria, Northern Spain
817. Visit the Chauvet Cave in the Ardèche département, southern France
818. Visit the Tower of London and see the Queen's Crown Jewels
819. Walk on the white limestone streets of Dubrovnik, Croatia
820. Walk the Berlin Wall
821. Walk on the black rock beaches of Iceland
822. Walk through the Plitvice Lakes in Croatia
823. Watch a Tennis Match at Wimbledon
824. Watch a road race in Monaco

North America

825. Act like an immigrant seeking the US on the ferry to the Statue of Liberty
826. Attend Coachella at the Empire Polo Club in Indio, California
827. Attend Mardi Gras in New Orleans
828. Attend a film premier in Hollywood
829. Attend a luau in Hawaii and wear a Lei
830. Be a part of a Las Vegas Show
831. Be amazed by the Grand Canyon
832. Bike down Haleakala in Hawaii
833. Board down an active volcano in Nicaragua
834. Buy a diamond at Tiffany's in NYC
835. Camp under the stars in Moab, Utah
836. Celebrate the ball drop on NYE at Central Park Square
837. Chase a tornado across the American Midwest
838. Check out art at the Metropolitan Museum of Art in NYC
839. Cheer on the racers at the Indy 500
840. Climb the Haiku Stairs of Oahu in Hawaii
841. Climb to the top of a Fourteener in Colorado
842. Come up with the next big thing on a tour of Google headquarters
843. Commit to doing the Half-Dome ascent in Yosemite National Park
844. Cry at the Holocaust Museum in Washington, DC
845. Dance at Burning Man Festival in Los Angeles
846. Dive in the ruins at Tulum, Mexico
847. Drive the road to Hana in Hawaii
848. Find a name on the Vietnam Wall
849. Find your train in Grand Central Station in NYC
850. Float in hot air balloons at the Albuquerque International Balloon Fiesta
851. Get a thrill on the Edgewalk CN Tower in Ontario
852. Get lost in the Grand Tetons
853. Get lost on the grounds of the Biltmore Estate in North Carolina
854. Get your groove on at a blues bar in Chicago
855. Go for a jog through Central Park
856. Hang out with the animals in San Diego zoo
857. Have "High Tea" at the Plaza Hotel in New York, or perhaps at Fortnum & Mason in London
858. Hike the Appalachian trail
859. Hike through Buckskin Gulch in Utah
860. Hold a balloon at the Macy's Thanksgiving Day Parade
861. Hold onto a cable car in San Francisco
862. Hug the Redwoods in California
863. Hum the Full House theme song while in San Francisco
864. Ice skate at Rockefeller Center
865. Meet a Mayan Shaman in Honduras
866. Mimic the faces at Mount Rushmore
867. Observe the pros at the Masters
868. Participate in the Empire State Building Run Up (you have to run up 86 flights of stairs)
869. Pay homage to the dead at the Dia De Los Muertos Festival in Mexico City
870. Pay your respects at the 9/11 Memorial
871. Pick a wand at Harry Potter World
872. Plan a trip to DC during the National Cherry Blossom Festival
873. Play the slots in Vegas
874. Play volleyball at Coney Island Boardwalk
875. Put your hand on the Washington Monument
876. Rent an apartment in New York which overlooks Central Park for three months
877. Ride a bike through Monument Mall in DC
878. Ride in a classic car in Havana, Cuba
879. Ride the largest observatory wheel in the world in Vegas

880. Ride the only hybrid ferry in San Francisco over to visit Alcatraz
881. Ride on the subway in NYC
882. Rock out to a concert at Red Rock Ampitheater
883. Scream on a ride at Universal Studios
884. Search for Wile E Coyote at Monument Valley
885. Search for your favorite celebrity's star in Hollywood
886. See a Broadway play in NYC
887. Sit down next to the Lincoln Memorial
888. Sit in the stands at the Super Bowl
889. Snorkel off the coast of Belize
890. Snowboard on Whistler Mountain in Canada
891. Spend a week on Necker Island (Richard Branson's island)
892. Splash the spectators on Splash Mountain at Disneyland
893. Spot a celebrity in Los Angeles, CA
894. Spot an alligator on a tour of the Everglades National Park
895. Stamp your passport at all National Parks in the US
896. Stand in awe of the Garden of the Gods
897. Stand in every Olympic park
898. Stand in the geographical center of the US in Kansas
899. Stand in the beauty of the Royal Gorge in Colorado
900. Stand next to Multnomah Falls in Oregon
901. Stand under the Hollywood Sign
902. Stargaze in Borrego Springs, California
903. Step foot in every country in North America
904. Swim in Mexico's Yucatan cenotes
905. Swim in the five Great Lakes in North America
906. Swim with dolphins in the Caribbean
907. Take a road trip to New England in the fall
908. Take your picture in front of the Hollywood sign
909. Taste a margarita during Cinco de Mayo in Mexico
910. Throw Beads at Mardi Gras
911. Time Old Faithful's eruption in Yellowstone
912. Tour every Smithsonian museum
913. View NYC from the top of the Statue of Liberty
914. Visit all of the state capitals wearing a t-shirt from that state
915. Visit NASA headquarters
916. Visit all 50 US States
917. Walk behind the falls at Niagra Falls
918. Walk on Beale Street in Memphis
919. Walk the steps of Chichen Itza
920. Watch a movie at the Sundance Film Festival in Utah
921. Zipline in Costa Rica

Oceania

922. Act like a Hobbit in New Zealand and visit the places where they filmed "The Lord of the Rings"
923. Catch a wave surfing in the Pacific Ocean
924. Climb the Sydney Harbor Bridge
925. Drive the Great Ocean Road in Australia
926. Hug a Koala bear in Australia
927. Practice your Australian accent on a tour of the Australian Outback
928. Relax on a beach in Tahiti
929. Sail New Zealand's Islands
930. Scrutinize an Opera at the Sydney Opera House
931. See the beautiful fish at the Great Barrier Reef
932. Sleep in an overwater bungalow in Bora Bora
933. Spend two weeks in Fiji
934. Zorbing in New Zealand

Random

935. Stand at the South Pole
936. Step foot on all seven continents
937. Step foot on the moon
938. Swim in all five oceans
939. Touch the North Pole
940. Visit all of the natural wonders of the world and write down what makes them beautiful
941. Visit the five longest rivers in the world
942. Visit every UNESCO World Heritage site in your favorite country

South America/Antartica

943. Attend Carnival in Rio de Janeiro
944. Buy extravagant items in Buenos Aires
945. Catch mist at Angel Falls in Venezuela
946. Cross the Panama Canal
947. Dance the tango in Argentina
948. Discover Santuario de Las Lajas
949. Find the statues of Easter Island
950. Hike the Inca trail in Peru
951. Hike the trails at Machu Picchu
952. Hold your arms out at the Christ the Redeemer statue in Rio de Janeiro
953. Jump for joy at the base of Patagonia
954. Kayak in the Amazon Rainforest
955. Pet a penguin in Antarctica
956. Reflect at Salar de Uyuni in Bolivia
957. Scope out Lake Tititaca in Bolivia
958. Ski the Andes

959. Spy on a giant iguana in the Galapagos Islands
960. Step foot in every country in South America
961. Swim in the world's largest swimming pool San Alfonso del Mar in Algarrobo, Chile
962. Swing at the end of the world in Ecuador
963. Thirst for water at the Atacama Desert - the driest place on Earth
964. Touch the bottom of the earth at Tierra del Fuego
965. Unexpectedly discover Kaieteur Falls, Guyana
966. Visit Angel Falls, Venezuela

VOLUNTEER

967. Anonymously buy a stranger's lunch
968. Become a lifeguard and save a life
969. Become an organ donor on your license
970. Build a house with Habitat for Humanity
971. Build a school for an impoverished community
972. Buy 100 gift cards and hand them out to strangers
973. Contact a company you like just to compliment them
974. Donate blood
975. Donate your hair for someone who has cancer
976. Dress up as Santa Claus at Christmas and give away gifts
977. Entertain the elderly at a nursing home
978. Have a meal with homeless person
979. Help an endangered/injured animal
980. Help deliver a child
981. Help dig a well in a foreign country
982. Help save someone's life on a medical missions trip
983. Help someone check something off of their bucket list
984. Hold someone's hand when they die
985. Hug a child in an orphanage
986. Leave a 100% tip for a server
987. Leave a note for a stranger
988. Listen to stories from the elderly at a nursing home
989. Live like a homeless person for a week
990. Read books to a group of school children
991. Save someone's life
992. Send a care package to a soldier
993. Serve food in a soup kitchen
994. Sing Christmas carols in your neighborhood in July
995. Share a meal with a homeless person
996. Teach someone (who is not your child) to read
997. Teach someone something you know a lot about
998. Volunteer abroad for a month
999. Volunteer at a soup kitchen with your family
1000. Volunteer for a political campaign
1001. Volunteer once a week for an entire year

This list of 1001 bucket list items were made in collaboration with the following all-stars:

Kristin, Jane, Rachel Mayo, Neha Ghelani, Kyle the Intern, Philip the New Intern, Roy the Golden, Murr Daddy, Floyd Hinman, Zach Gamble, Elizabeth Leppek, Alison Grendahl, Alyssa Ross, Lisa Naomi Johnson, Beth Matson Glasoe, Amy M Loerke, Stephanie Stenger Jones, Linda Ritzer Wearne, Brandon Bell, Hailey Pace Thomas, Matt Ham, Cara Duncan, Ronne Rock, Charles Balan, Lily Kreitinger, Mitch Stephens, Jamie Foster Ballard, Joe Givens, Tracy Dusek, Shayla Golden, Beth Stauffer, Jenn Murr, Kay Helm, Melissa Reagan, Alyssa Horton, Christina Fast-Lebeiko, Kim Wright, Heather Turner, Diane Morrow Kondos, Christy Bouchard, Emily Mocha, Amanda Holland, Jennifer Chessmore, Kerri McDaris, Anita Hylton Thompson, Zakariya Rafiq Rajpari, Scott Cuzzo, Taryn Starkey, Shelia Unger Fritts, Mark Collard, Jean Swienton Brassfield, Andrea Williams, Eric Crittenden, Kyrsten Gamble, Anna Floit, Jane Tuttle, Jennifer Allison, Bethany Joy Johnson, Julie DeVisser, Jamie Cowan, Haley Stocks, Justin Lane Douillard, Brandon Nickell, Barry Steveson, Kevin Dotson, Arthur Smith, Jake Smith, Randy Langley, Trae Ratliff, Kris Simpson, David Dollar, Tamarah West, May Bohon, Jami Murphy, Janeen Kilgore, Paige Garvin, Sarah Kusler, Amanda Martin, Will Jenkins, Ronei Harden, Sarah Johnson, Diana Nathan, Lacey Steveson, Linda Spyres, Audra Brown, Amanda Russell, Peggy Glenn, Kyle Schaefer, and Brian Hope.

LIVE YOUR LIST
INTENTIONAL LEADERSHIP

RYAN ELLER & JERROD MURR

Practical tips, stories, & resources for a better you.

The *Live Your List* Show with Jerrod Murr and Ryan Eller is a weekly podcast dedicated to intentional leadership, personal development, and living with purpose. It is fun, engaging, fresh, and all about figuring out how to *Live Your List*.

Find us online at *ryaneller.com/live-your-list-show*
Listen to us on iTunes and Stitcher.
Join the conversation on Facebook at *facebook.com/groups/liveyourlist*
Follow us on Twitter *@Live_Your_List* and Instagram *@liveyourlistok*

PLAYLISTS LISTENED TO WHILE WRITING THIS BOOK + RECOMMENDATIONS

Throwback Workout - Neha Ghelani

Summer Hits of the 90s - Shelby Gamble

Disney on Ice - Cousin Amy

Conway Twitty - Jerrod Murr

Limp Bizkit's *Greatest Hits* - Me from 1998

Imagine Dragons - Philip the New Intern

Acoustic Punk - Hailey Pace Thomas

Timber Timbre Radio - Floyd Hinman

Most Beautiful Songs in the World - Kyle the Intern

90s Boy Bands - Rachel Mayo

All Day by Girl Talk! - Heather Turner

Dreamland: An Exercise in Imagination - Brandon Richards

90s and 2000s Hip Hop - Cousin Patrick

NSYNC & Backstreet Boys - Emeka Nnaka

Chill Hits - Alison Grendenhall

Summer Nights - Jon Levensque

50 Cent, Eminem, & NWA - Zach Gamble

Lindsey Stirling - Tanner Dean Garrison

Wonder Woman: Music of Destiny - May Bohan

Head and the Heart - Melissa Pierce Harris

Starred - Cousin Austin

Bay City Jams - Seth Clark

2Cellos - BeLinda Creech

Milano Music - Mary Ann Rouse

Party Country - Big Kat & Catoosa HS Class of 2018

Explosion in the Sky - Kat Nguyen

Greensky Bluegrass - Casey Dillard

Glen Hansard Complete - Bryson Williams

Infinite Acoustic - Kristin Stowe

Frank Sinatra - Ronda McLelland

John Mayer - Paige Davis

Cereus Bright - Kaitlin Grant

Trampled by Turtles - Jordan Cox

Paul Simon - Eva Silvia Lozano

Mom's Favorites 865 - Suzi Sullivan

All Time Greatest - Russell Herrin

80s Smash Hits - Justin Douillard

L.I.S.T.E.N. - Scott Robertson

Study Music - Bobby Hill

Backstreet Boys - Emily Mocha

Perfect Places - Caleb Eustler

N-D - Wes Horton

90s R&B - Billinda Harvey

Blane's Mix - Blane Hoag

ABOUT THE AUTHOR
RYAN ELLER

Ryan Eller is a dreamer of dreams and a music maker. He is the cofounder of Paradigm Shift, a company that facilitates leadership training across the world. Ryan has led workshops, keynotes, and trainings in over 45 states and on four continents. Ryan has the goal of hosting a leadership training in all 50 states, in 100 countries, and on all seven continents.

He is a member of several large non-profit boards across the nation, has advocated for educational aspiration in Washington D.C., and is a proud champion of the millennial generation.

Ryan spent seven years as Grant Coordinator for Educational Talent Search at Northeastern State University, the college where he obtained a bachelor's degree in Mass Communication and master's in Higher Education Administration. He is currently in the process of earning his doctorate in education from the University of Arkansas.

Ryan has danced with Miss America, won a game show, got lost on the Great Wall of China, broken a world record, and married way out of his league. He has jumped out of planes, walked with lions, and jumped off of waterfalls.

Most importantly, Ryan is married to his college sweetheart, Kristin, and they have the cutest children ever - Jane & Caleb. Things he loves and are often found talking about (*in no particular order*): Kristin, Jane, Caleb, the OKC Thunder, a strong Nick Collison screen, his grandpa's farm, OU college football, his huge family, dreaming big dreams, breakfast — specifically biscuits and gravy — retelling a story, running, *LOST*, checking something off of his bucket list, traveling the world, achieving a goal, and meeting new people.

He is always trying to *Live his List* and wants you to do the same!

I wouldn't want to live my list with anyone else.
Love you, sweetheart.